G000069463

South of France

Jonathan Healey

Series editor: Patrick Matthews

DISCOVERING WINE COUNTRY
SOUTH OF FRANCE
by Jonathan Healey

FIrst published in Great Britain in 2005
by Mitchell Beazley, an imprint of Octopus Publishing Group Limited,
2–4 Heron Quays, London E14 4JP.

A CIP catalogue record for this book is available from the British Library.

ISBN: 1 84533 037 4

The author and publishers will be grateful for any information which will assist them in keeping future editions up-to-date. Although all reasonable care has been taken in the preparation of this book, neither the publishers nor the author can accept any liability for any consequences arising from the use thereof, or the information contained therein.

Photographs by Victoria McTernan
Map creation by Encompass Graphics

Commissioning Editor Hilary Lumsden
Executive Art Editor Yasia Williams-Leedham
Senior Designer Tim Pattinson
Managing Editor Julie Sheppard
Editors Susanna Forbes and Margaret Rand
Designer Gaelle Lochner
Index Hilary Bird
Production Gary Hayes

Typeset in Futura and Sabon

Printed and bound by Toppan Printing Company in China

ACKNOWLEDGEMENTS

I would like to thank Hilary Lumsden and the team at Mitchell Beazely for having faith in this book and for putting it together so well; Yasia Williams-Leedham and Gaelle Lochner for the stylish design; Julie Shepphard, Margaret Rand, and Susanna Forbes for their tight editing; Tory for her superb photographs; and Tom Coulson for making the maps so clear. Thanks also to the staff of the Conseils Interprofessionnels des Vins of Provence, Languedoc, and Roussillon for pointing me off the beaten track: Anne Sophie Carlin, Christophe Logeais and Eric Aracil. Most of all, I would like to thank the producers featured in this book for their time, dedication, and passion.

Contents

How to use this book

Discovering Wine Country is all about getting you from the page to the producer. Each chapter covers a specific winemaking region of interest, and includes a map of the area featured, with places of interest marked using the symbols below. The leading wine producers mentioned are all given a map grid reference so you can see exactly where they are.

The maps include key features to help you navigate your way round the routes, but they are not intended to replace detailed road maps, or indeed detailed vineyard maps, normally available from local tourist offices or the local wine bureaus (*see below, right*).

It wouldn't be practical to mark each and every grower on the maps. Instead the sign ❧ means that an area or village is home to at least one recommended wine producer. The wine regions covered are packed with other points of interest for the wine enthusiast but that are unrelated to actual wine purchasing. These are shown as ⛪ Sometimes this includes growers who don't sell direct but whose status is such that they will be on any wine-lover's itinerary. Exceptional restaurants are marked ⦿ and towns and villages where there's an Office de Tourism are marked ℹ which is especially useful for finding *gîtes* and campsites.

Quick reference map symbols
❧ recommended wine producer
⛪ wine tourist site
★ tourist attraction
⦿ recommended restaurant
ℹ tourist information centre

 named wine region(s)

 author's suggested wine route(s) to follow, with information about how long the route is and any other useful tips.

 scale bar

north compass

Boxed information
the contact details of hotels, restaurants, tourist information, hire shops, transport facilities, and other points of interest.

wine-related information as well as the author's selection of the top growers to visit in the specific area featured, including contact details, a map reference, and a price indicator (due to space constraints in this book some of the growers are listed in a separate section at the back of the book):
inexpensive: <€5
moderate: €5–10
expensive: €10–20

Local wine bureaus

CIVL (Conseil Interprofessionnel des Vins du Languedoc)
www.languedoc-wines.com

CIVR (Conseil Interprofessionnel des Vins du Roussillon)
www.vinsduroussillon.com/us/index.php

CIVP (Conseil Interprofessionnel des Vins du Provence)
www.cotes-de-provence.fr/civp/

Introduction

What could be more pleasurable than enjoying fine wines while discovering the hidden delights of one of the world's most famous and glamorous regions – the south of France? There's never been a better time to go, too. Provence, Languedoc and Roussillon – France's viticultural "New World" – are producing wines of such quality, at very reasonable prices, that they're becoming hard to beat. And with the advent of low-cost airlines, the south of France is more accessible than ever.

Exploring the south of France

This book will help you explore the south of France and make the most of your time on holiday. It takes you into the cellars of talented winemakers across the south and introduces you to their history and their wines; it tells you what to buy and how to get your wines home. And, to help you discover the region's wine country in full, there are twenty maps and detailed itineraries plus descriptions of other local attractions not to be missed – many of which are off the beaten tourist tracks. There are recommendations of where to stay, where to eat, and how best to get around, too. It's the perfect companion to a wine-oriented trip.

Back to basics

As well as essential tourist information, in the first part of this guide you'll learn about the wines – and how to taste them. This book explains which grape varieties are grown, how the wines are made, and gives you lots of useful tips for how to go about visiting local winemakers. You'll also discover the traditions of the people, their festivals and their local gastronomy. In short, you'll come to appreciate what makes the south of France so special.

Location, location, location

The second part of the book begins in the hidden vineyards of Bellet in the hills overlooking fabulous Nice. It takes you to châteaux and perched villages across rolling Provençal landscapes, and along the most celebrated coastline in the world to St-Tropez and the stunning Ile de Porquerolles. Along the way, you'll sample wines around beautiful Aix-en-Provence and spectacular Les Baux, and discover vineyards set amid landscapes made famous by Cézanne and Van Gogh.

Then you'll encounter the south of France's best-kept secret: the unspoiled departments of Languedoc and Roussillon, where you'll be guided through mountain and coastal vineyards around Nîmes, Montpellier, Narbonne, Carcassonne, and Perpignan. Along the way, you'll discover the Languedoc's rich Roman and medieval heritage – including the impressive Nîmes arena, lively Montpellier's old town, Carcassonne's fairy-tale citadel, the famous Cathar castles of the Corbières, and the impressive abbeys of Lagrasse and Fontfroide west of Narbonne.

Finally, you'll discover Roussillon with its delicious sweet wines, long sandy beaches, and vibrant Catalan culture which is centred on Perpignan, France's sunniest, most southerly, and most cosmopolitan city. Along the way, you'll encounter outstanding Romanesque art; explore the landscapes that inspired Picasso and Matisse; and visit vineyards dominated by Mont Canigou, one of the highest peaks in the Pyrénées. Your journey ends amid the precipitous vineyards around the pretty ports of Collioure and Banyuls-sur-Mer, near the Spanish border, where the foothills of the Pyrénées plunge spectacularly into the Mediterranean.

LEFT *The port of Collioure: the hills behind boast some of France's steepest vineyards.*

Understanding the South of France

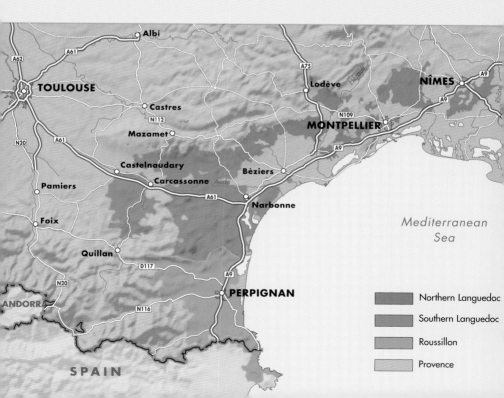

Albi

A62   A61

TOULOUSE

Castres
N112

Mazamet

N20   A61

Castelnaudary
Carcassonne   Aude

Pamiers

A61

Foix

Quillan

D117

N20

ANDORRA

N116

SPAIN

A75

Lodève

Hérault

NÎMES   A9

A9

N109

MONTPELLIER

A9

Béziers

Narbonne

Mediterranean Sea

A9

PERPIGNAN

Rhône

Northern Languedoc

Southern Languedoc

Roussillon

Provence

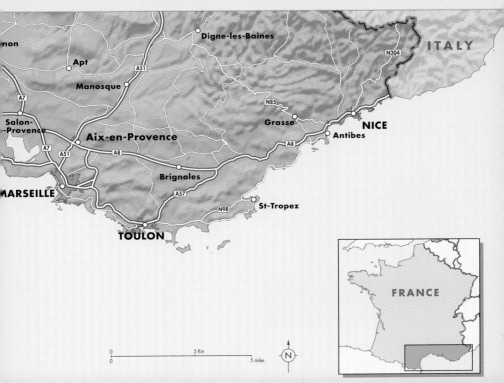

non

Apt

A51

Manosque

A7

Salon-
Provence

A7

A51

Aix-en-Provence

A8

MARSEILLE

Brignoles

A57

TOULON

Digne-les-Baines

N204

ITALY

N85

Grasse

Antibes

NICE

A8

St-Tropez

N98

0   5 Km
0   5 miles

N

FRANCE

What makes the south of France unique?

A part from bags of sunshine, spectacular scenery, a Gallo-Roman history; medieval citadels; picturesque abbeys; rolling hills of lavender, sunflowers, and olives; scented *garrigue* scrubland; stunted oaks and umbrella pines; a famous *art de vivre;* and beautiful cities like Nice, Aix-en-Provence, Montpellier, Carcassonne, and Perpignan, what makes the south of France unique? It's the wines – or rather, their extraordinary variety and individuality.

Côtes de Provence – more than pink

This guide begins near the Italian border in the terraced hills behind Nice with the whites of Bellet. This appellation has just a dozen or so producers. While the lemony whites are made from Rolle, most producers also make reds and rosés from the rare Braque grape, with its distinctive rosewater aromas.

Travelling west along the coast, Frèjus is at the eastern end of the Côtes de Provence, an appellation firmly associated with thirst-quenchingly crisp, fruity rosés. They're frivolous and fun, but you can take the Cabernet-based reds and the tropical Sémillon-based whites seriously.

The varied Côtes de Provence vineyards include the cool Haut Pays in the Gorges du Verdon foothills, the rolling Vallée Interiéure north of the wooded Maures Massif, the coastal Bordure Maritime, and the beautiful Ile de Porquerolles. There's also a pocket of Côtes de Provence, the Bassin de Beausset, between Bandol and Cassis.

Two special appellations

Bandol and Cassis are pretty ports with very different wines. Bandol has a reputation for dense, Mourvèdre-based, oak-aged reds that take a decade to soften up. The vineyards, on an amphitheatre of slopes behind the town, are some of the most spectacular in Provence. Those of Cassis are planted along the highest cliff in France, the dramatic Cap Canaille. As Provence's poet laureate, Frédéric Mistral, said: "If you've seen Paris, but not Cassis, you ain't seen nothing." Cassis produces a slightly salty, floral white that goes with the local seafood.

Shades of Cézanne

North of Bandol, the Coteaux Varois vineyards cover some of the most attractive Provençal landscapes. The best reds emphasise Syrah and are extremely good value. West of the Coteaux Varois, between Aix-en-Provence and St-Maximin, are the Ste-Victoire vineyards. Cézanne's beloved Montagne Ste-Victoire dominates the skyline here. This is rosé country, but you'll find Clairette and Rolle-based whites and fruit-driven reds, too.

Training your Palette

West of Ste-Victoire, just outside Aix-en-Provence, is the Palette appellation. There are three significant producers and the wines are commonly oak-aged, expensive, and worth seeking out (see p.63). The sprawling Coteaux d'Aix-en-Provence appellation west of Palette specialises in early-drinking reds and some vins de garde, wines more suitable for ageing.

To the west of Provence, the Les Baux vineyards cover slopes on the craggy Alpilles Massif, which rises out of the Rhône delta north of the Camargue wetlands. Organic viticulture is common here and the focus is on rich, spicy reds based on Mourvèdre or Syrah, depending on whether you're on the northern or southern slopes. These are the most westerly vineyards in Provence.

ABOVE *The architecturally rich town of Caunes-Minervois made its fortune from the nearby marble quarries.*

LEFT *The neo-gothic Château de Montpezat is set in attractive parkland beside the river Peyne west of Pézenas.*

Across the Rhône and into the Languedoc

The Languedoc and the gently sloping Costières de Nîmes are across the Rhône. Good-value, light and fruity primeur-style reds, made for drinking young, characterise the Costières, with a pocket of Clairette-based whites around Bellegarde. West are the Grès de Montpellier vineyards, which make immediately attractive reds. The jutting Pic St-Loup, north of Montpellier, is a Languedoc icon as well as a trendy cru producing world-class reds and elegant rosés.

Just outside Montpellier's western suburbs some of the best Coteaux du Languedoc reds are made in the pebbly chalk and limestone of the St-Georges-d'Orques vineyards. Honey-sweet Muscats of Mireval and Frontignan grow in vineyards facing the sea. Down the coast, beside the Bassin de Thau, is the white Picpoul de Pinet appellation, based on the Picpoul grape. The wine's lemony tang goes perfectly with the local seafood.

Fashionable *crus*

North of Picpoul are the cooler, hilly vineyards of Pézenas, Cabrières, and the Terrasses du Larzac. The latter incorporates

ABOVE *Perpignan's medieval masterpiece, the graceful Loge de la Mer (1397), houses one of the town's smartest cafés.*

RIGHT *Originally a twelfth-century Cistercian abbey, the Château des Garcinières in Cogolin, Côtes de Provence, was turned into a home by the Counts of Grimaldi in the eighteenth century.*

the trendy red *crus* of St-Saturnin and Montpeyroux, while the Clairette du Languedoc appellation covers half of the Cabrières terroir. Cabrières has a reputation for deeply coloured Cinsault-based rosés. St-Saturnin is known for its young wines, its *vin de primeur*. while Montpeyroux specializes in rich, full-bodied reds. Pézenas' wines are similar to those from Faugères.

Faugères and St-Chinian are noted for their minerally reds and rosés. West of St-Chinian, the Minervois covers terraces on the Montagne Noire's southern slopes and produces generous, fruit-driven wines and superior sweet Muscats.

The Atlantic influence

The Languedoc's most westerly terroirs, Cabardès and Malepère, are influenced by the Atlantic. The new, good-value appellations emphasising Cabernet Sauvignon occur west of Minervois and north and south of Carcassonne. In the hilly, upper Aude Valley, south of the massif of Malepère, is the sparkling white Limoux appellation. Chardonnay, Mauzac, and Pinot Noir all do well in these high-altitude vineyards.

South of Minervois is the Corbières, the fourth-largest appellation in France. The vineyards cover rugged limestone mountains where spicy Carignan-based reds are made. East of Narbonne, on a massif that was an island in the middle ages, is the quality Coteaux du Languedoc *cru* of La Clape.

Heading south again

France's most southerly vineyards are near the Spanish border in Roussillon, where the Pyrénées meet the Med. Famous for its sweet fortified *vins doux naturels*, the region is also a source of bold southern reds, especially around the pretty port of Collioure.

The people and the place

The south of France is both the cradle of French viticulture and its "New World" – it's where French wine culture had its beginning, and it's where the most exciting developments are taking place today. No other French region can boast such a long association with winemaking – not Bordeaux, not Burgundy, not Champagne. Twenty-six centuries ago, the Greeks initiated the enthusiastic locals into the culture of wine. They planted what were probably the first cultivated vines in France around their port colony of Marsilia, present-day Marseille, and also imported enormous quantities of wine.

What the Romans did

The Romans vastly expanded the region's vineyards. They founded the ports of Forum Julii, present-day Frèjus in Provence, and Narbonne in the Languedoc; by now France was exporting large quantities of wine to Italy. The end of the Roman Empire did little to diminish viticultural prosperity. With the establishment of the great Benedictine and Cistercian abbeys, winemaking in the south expanded dramatically. In the middle ages there were more than fifty abbeys across the region.

Transport solutions

With the opening of the Canal du Midi linking the Atlantic to the Mediterranean in 1681 (these days it's a UNESCO World Heritage Site), new markets appeared. The advent of the railways brought still more.

Many châteaux in this guide date from this hugely profitable period, when wines from the south quenched the thirst of miners and factory workers in the north, even if the quality was nothing to be proud of.

Living history

Yet, there's plenty of pride in the region's heritage. Motorways are named after Roman roads and many domaines trace their origins to antiquity, or to medieval times. There's even one winery in the Languedoc still making wine the Roman way – Mas des Tourelles near Nîmes. People also take pride in being Catalan (from Roussillon) or Occitan (from Languedoc and Provence).

These days, that pride is translating itself into something of a renaissance. A new breed of passionate, ambitious and restless winemaker is demonstrating that the south can make world-class wines. They've embraced new cellar technologies and planted more aromatic varieties in the vineyards.

The New World comes to France

Not for nothing is the south considered France's "New World". It's not uncommon to meet young *vignerons* who have gained winemaking experience in Chile, South Africa, Australia or California. Today, there are around 200 Australians producing wine in the region. English, German, and Dutch winemakers have also been spotted alongside newcomers from Champagne, Burgundy, and Bordeaux. These winemakers don't look to Brussels for subsidies; they look around the world for new markets.

The terroir tradition

Many of the new winemakers, however, retain an appreciation for what makes the south unique – its terroir. In fact, if one thing distinguishes France's "New World" from its New World competitors, it's this traditional recognition of the importance of soil, terrain, and microclimate.

But perhaps the most conspicuous characteristic of winemakers in the south, and the people in general, is their spirit of independence. Often the most intriguing wines are made by those *vignerons* who flout officialdom and appellation rules. Unburdened by history and received wisdom, these are the ones to watch.

THE GREEN SOUTH

The south leads the way in organic and, increasingly, Biodynamic viticulture. This is particularly the case in Les Baux and the Coteaux Varois (both in Provence).

There are several shades of green: light green *lutte raisonnée* (minimal use of chemicals); greener *lutte intégrée* (some biological treatments, like predators to combat pests); dark green *biologique* (organic); and mystic green *Biodynamique* (inspired by spiritual scientist Rudolf Steiner, in which the movements of the moon and planets determine when to apply organic and Biodynamic treatments).

Seasons and festivals

Great wines, it is often said, are made in the vineyard, and this is where a top *vigneron* spends most of his or her time, anticipating and working with the seasons. The aim is to produce ripe, healthy, and concentrated grapes that can be transformed into the best wine possible after the harvest. The vagaries of the weather, the appetite of pests during the growing cycle, and the *vigneron*'s decision regarding the yield of the vines will all affect the quality of the grapes (high yields give less concentrated juice), but the fact remains that judicious vineyard work pays off in the cellar.

Party time
The *vigneron*'s year is not all work and no play. There are countless festivals throughout the wine year. Some are local; at other times, whole regions unite in a celebration of wine and, of course, food. Some festivals last a day, others a weekend and in the Languedoc's sparkling white wine capital of Limoux, the carnival lasts from January to March.

Harvest, and its festival
The most visible event in the wine year is the harvest, which generally happens in September and October. Pickers pack the vineyards and slow-moving tractors laden with sweet-smelling grapes clog the roads. Harvesting generally lasts two months, which is the difference in ripening between the earliest varieties, like Chardonnay, and late-ripeners like Mourvèdre.

The harvest festival – Fête des Vendanges – is a perennial feature of the calendar and typically involves the whole community and any visitors who care to join in the fun. There's a lively harvest festival in Banyuls-sur-Mer in Roussillon during the last weekend in October. There are barbeques on the beach, wine-basket-carrying, and barrel-tossing competitions (a sort of south of France Highland Games), plus music and dancing.

Celebrating the new wines
The life cycle of the vine recommences following the harvest. While the *vigneron* gets busy making wine in November and December, the vines change colour and begin to enter a dormant period. As the sap descends into the roots with the onset of cold

LEFT *Café life is a big part of the south of France's famous* art de vivre.

BELOW *Ornate statues, like this one in Notre-Dame-de-Londres, add colour to otherwise austere Romanesque churches.*

weather, the first of the year's young wines, its *vins primeurs*, are ready for bottling. This is the occasion for another bout of festivities. These light-bodied wines don't claim to be serious, and many *primeur* bottles bear colourful, festive labels. On the second weekend of November, the *vignerons* of Les Baux invite producers from the neighbouring appellations and host a *dégustation* (tasting) for the public.

Just in time for Christmas...

The *primeur* season is barely over before the first of the year's new sweet Muscats hit the shelves. In Roussillon, they're labelled "Muscat de Noël" and they appear at the beginning of December. Inevitably, this is the occasion for more merry-making. For the *vigneron*, this is also the time to tidy up in the vineyard, to pull up any exhausted vines, and to cut away any dead wood. It's a time to plough in fertilizers and to heap up earth around the vines' roots to protect them against occasional winter frosts. It's also a time to repair stakes, wires, and terrace walls, and to replace soils washed away by the rain.

Competitive pruning

January and February are important pruning months. Fires are a common way to dispose of cuttings and it's not unusual to see smoke mingling with the early morning mist above the vineyards. Vine-pruning competitions are a feature of the winter, although you need to be a real enthusiast to enjoy them. Pruning continues until the the sap rises in the spring.

January also sees celebrations associated with St-Vincent, the patron saint of wine. *Vignerons* in the Coteaux d'Aix-en-Provence put down their secateurs for their hugely popular Fête de St-Vincent in the village of Coudoux around the second Sunday in January. There's music, dancing, and a parade. Meanwhile, in the *cave*, rosés or whites from the previous year are bottled and reds might be racked off into clean barrels.

Springtime work

Vines come back to life in March and typically begin to bud between the second week in March and the second week in April, depending on the variety and where you are. Within

FINDING A FESTIVAL

When travelling around the wine regions in this guide, **check with the local tourist offices for details of wine festivals** associated with the seasons' activities. In the south of France you're seldom more than a month away from some festival in which wine features.

days of budding, the young stalks, leaves and tendrils sprout, and a green haze covers the vineyards. This is another time for ploughing, this time to aerate the soil and to expose the base of the vine to the sunshine. More tidying up takes place in the vineyards, plus some weeding and, once the possibility of frosts has diminished, replanting can take place.

When the vegetative cycle starts again in May, some protective treatments may be applied against the various forms of mildew and pests. Increasingly, natural predators are introduced into the vineyards to combat pests and to avoid the undesirable use of chemical pesticides. With the beneficial climate in the south – warm and dry, which reduces the incidence of vine disease – *vignerons* are increasingly practising organic viticulture.

Flowering – a time of worry

Flower buds begin to appear around the middle of May and flowering proper is underway by early June. It takes ten to fourteen days for the tiny white flowers to "set" as they begin their transformation into nascent grapes. This is a critical period during which cold temperatures, excessive humidity, heavy rains or high winds are extremely detrimental to the crop.

In July, some leaves are removed to expose the grapes to more sun. In August, with the grapes well grown, some bunches are removed to reduce the final crop and increase intensity. Then the green berries change colour, and soon the harvest comes round again. The *vigneron* is in the vineyard making almost daily checks on the sweetness, acidity, and concentration of the grapes before the date to start picking is set. And though this is a busy and stressful time, there's always a sense of expectation and much excited talk about the potential of the year's wines.

LEFT Brins de muguet, *small bouquets of lily-of-the-valley are traditionally offered on May 1 to bestow good luck.*

BELOW Cézanne liked to paint *the countryside around Château Crémade in Le Tholonet, Provence.*

Knowing the wines

The south of France's appellation wines are blends of mainly Mediterranean grape varieties which have a long history in the region. The Greeks brought some of them over two millennia ago. Grapes native to other parts of France are also grown for some wines. For example, Cabernet Sauvignon from Bordeaux, and Chardonnay from Burgundy perform well here and are permitted in a number of appellations.

Why learn about grapes?

Grape varieties contribute more than anything else to the flavour and character of a wine, and knowing something about them tells you much about the wines. Terroir, viticultural practices, and methods of vinification are each important, and weather can determine the success of a vintage, but ultimately different grape varieties produce wines of discernibly different character.

To understand the wines better, here's a brief introduction to the most commonly encountered grapes.

Red grapes

Cabernet Sauvignon This grape is the most widely recognized red grape in the world was brought to the south of France from Bordeaux in the second half of the twentieth century. It's an accommodating variety which produces an instantly recognizable wine wherever it's grown. The small, thick-skinned grapes give tannin, colour, and distinctive blackcurrant, licorice, chocolate, and "lead pencil" flavours, and wines that can age.

Carignan The most common variety in the south, this almost certainly originated in Spain. It produces wines high in acidity and tannins with a coarse, rustic smell of hot berries. Restraining the size of the crop, however, produces a warm, rich wine, strong in colour, extract, alcohol, and tannins.

Cinsault Another Mediterranean old-timer, Cinsault often complements Grenache and Carignan. The juice is low in tannin and alcohol but it gives stylish, supple, and soft ripe red-fruit flavours plus good acidity. It's the base wine for many lightly perfumed rosés.

RIGHT *Wild flowers in the vineyard, like these at Domaine du Petit Roubié near Pinet, often mean the estate is worked organically.*

BELOW *Wine labels don't always identify the grapes used, so it pays to ask.*

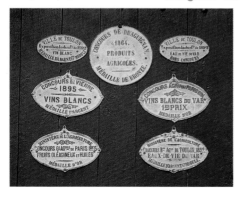

Grenache Noir This thin-skinned variety is frequently blended with Carignan. What it lacks in colour, acidity, and tannins, it makes up for in gutsy fruit and earthy flavours, bringing roundness, body, and alcoholic oomph to the blend.

Merlot This is now France's third most popular variety (after Carignan and Grenache). Merlot yields a fuller-bodied, less acidic and less tannic wine than Cabernet Sauvignon. It's also higher in alcohol. Because of its plump, soft, aromatic, velvety, and fruity appeal reminiscent of plums and fruitcake, it is sometimes called the Ribena of red wines.

Mourvèdre The full glories of Mourvèdre's rich, gamey, black-fruit flavours are seldom evident in its youth. Expect taut wines with great tannic strength that are most expressive with age.

Pinot Noir Pinot Noir is inextricably linked with the great red wines of Burgundy, where it has been cultivated for over 1,500 years. It's rarely found in vineyards in the south, but there is some Pinot Noir around Limoux in the Languedoc department of the Aude. It is sometimes blended into the local sparkling whites to give them more of a Champagne character, and it is also used to make a burgundy-style red with cherry, strawberry, raspberry, and violet aromas. Gamey and spicy accents evolve with age.

Syrah In France, the Rhône in particular specialises in this enormously popular variety. It gives structure and density and wines capable of ageing. They're usually dark in colour with complex aromas of brambles, forest fruits, musk, truffles, spices, and even tar.

Tibouren This quintessentially Provençal variety almost certainly arrived with the Greeks. It is prized for its ability to produce light, supple, and earthy rosés with distinctive scents of the *garrigue* and zesty white fruit flavours.

White grapes

Bourboulenc This variety is known as Malvoisie in Roussillon. It gives fine, full-bodied, golden, aromatic wine with a floral character, honeyed notes, and good acidity and alcohol. The best demonstrate considerable finesse and complexity.

Chardonnay Chardonnay was born in medieval France, but has been adopted across the south – and indeed worldwide. In the last twenty years it has become almost a brand for novice wine drinkers. It can be quite alcoholic, fairly low in acidity, with delicate aromas of tropical fruits, melon, peaches, vanilla, and hazelnuts. It can improve with age, too, and is often oak-aged. In Bellet it's blended with Rolle.

RIGHT *Knowing about grape varieties helps you discern a wine's aromas and flavours.*

BELOW *An appellation's Maison des Vins, like this one in the Coteaux Varois, is a good place to learn more about both grapes and wines.*

Chenin Blanc This versatile grape is found in Limoux, in the Languedoc department of the Aude, where it contributes acidity and distinctive honey and straw flavours to the local sparkling wines from Mauzac and Chardonnay. Elsewhere, it's commonly partnered with Sémillon or Sauvignon Blanc, but it can make a fine varietal wine in its own right.

Clairette On its own, Clairette wines tend to be flabby and alcoholic and to oxidize early. With distinctive apple aromas, it tends to be blended with Grenache Blanc, Ugni Blanc, and Marsanne in Cassis.

Grenache Blanc The juicy, sweet, yellow-green berries give soft, supple, and fruity wines that can be high in alcohol, though sometimes lacking in acidity. With careful vineyard work and fermentation in casks, the variety can produce richly aromatic and full-bodied wines worthy of oak ageing.

Macabeu Wines made from Macabeu have a herbal and floral character. They can be quite alcoholic, too, though lacking in acidity.

Marsanne This can make a light, elegant, aromatic, and fruity wine with some finesse. It typically gives almond paste, even glue, aromas to the bouquet, although the alcohol level sometimes gets the better of the acidity.

Mauzac In Limoux this variety is blended with Chardonnay and Chenin Blanc. Mauzac gives wines with aromas of dried apples and pears if it's not harvested too early.

Muscat There are numerous Muscats around but just two of them are important in the south of France: Muscat à Petits Grains and Muscat d'Alexandrie. The delicate Muscat à Petits Grains is regarded as the superior of the two, having more gentle grapey aromas with hints of orange blossom and honeysuckle. The resilient Muscat d'Alexandrie can easily overpower with its intense geranium and tomcat aromas. They're both used for making sweet wines but dry versions are increasingly common.

Picpoul The name Picpoul means "lip stinger" as the variety can produce a zesty, lemony, dry, and full-bodied wine with reliable levels of acidity, though it's not particularly high in alcohol. It's commonly partnered with Clairette.

Rolle A richly aromatic variety with distinctive floral, honey, pear, and citrus accents. Exotic fruits, pineapple, and almonds are also featured in its wines. Rolle has a useful balance of perfume, body, and acidity that takes wood fermentation and ageing well.

ABOVE *Grapes are picked when the balance between acidity, sweetness, and concentration is just right.*

Roussanne This is one of the finest French white grapes. The wines are elegant and complex, delicately floral, and memorably fragrant with refreshingly balanced levels of acidity and alcohol. Aromas of peonies, honeysuckle, apricots, the *garrigue*, and zesty herbal tea are not uncommon. It's often blended with Marsanne and Chardonnay, and it is rare to find it on its own.

Sauvignon Blanc Sauvignon Blanc is planted all over southwest France, particularly in Bergerac, but the undisputed French capital of Sauvignon Blanc is the Loire. Sauvignon Blanc has a distinctive flinty, smoky, steely, and sharply acidic flavour with aromas of asparagus, gooseberry, blackcurrant leaf, and freshly mown grass often cited (some even detect cat's pee). Above all, it's pale, dry, and bracing. In the south of France, it's found especially in Bandol and Cassis.

Sémillon This is the golden grape of southwest France and an important variety in Provence. It is productive and vigorous but rarely stars on its own. Its greatest strength is as a blending partner, commonly with Sauvignon Blanc and Chardonnay. It adds body and roundness, though not always aromatic complexity or acidity. Sémillon is capable of ageing and, when treated appropriately, adds honey and white flower accents to its partners. It would be more widespread in the south but for its lack of acidity when grown here.

Ugni Blanc France's most widely planted white grape variety probably came to France from Italy during the fourteenth century. It's a prolific cropper used to make cognac and armagnac and produces reliably light, acidic, and supple wines. The small, golden-coloured berries impart a distinctive yellow hue, although they're relatively low in alcohol and flavour. Limited yields increase the character of this often maligned variety.

Viognier The fashionable Viognier spent several centuries in the Rhône Valley before colonizing the south of France. It produces an elegant and distinctive wine: full-bodied, heady, high in alcohol and colour, with aromas of apricots, peaches, freesias, ginger, citrus, and musk. It also has an unctuous, creamy texture and should be drunk young because of its low acidity. It needs to be superripe to develop its characteristic aroma and flavour. Viognier is a reluctant cropper that produces small clusters of grapes.

Food and wine culture

Wine is drunk before, during and after meals in the south of France. Meals begin with an apéritif – either a sweet wine like a Muscat, or a *coupe*, a glass of sparkling wine – and end with a digestif, either another sweet wine such as Banyuls or a spirit. Meals are accompanied by whatever wine best suits the intervening *entrée* (the starter) and the *plat principal* (the main course). Wine culture in the south is thus inseparable from food culture. There's a strong sense of regional identity, too. Few restaurants in Roussillon, for instance, feature Provençal wines or dishes, and the converse is also true. Some restaurants propose menus based on local specialities, with food and wine choices made for you.

Local traditions

Eating here means Mediterranean cuisine. In Provence there's an Italian influence; in Roussillon the influence is Spanish. In the Languedoc, traditions are less well defined, and some village cafés can be uninspiring. In bigger towns, like Montpellier, a culinary renaissance is underway.

Strong, vibrant flavours

Although there are regional variations, you will encounter certain ingredients like olives, garlic, and tomatoes again and again. Aubergines, courgettes, red peppers, mushrooms, and onions are used to make the perennial favourite, *ratatouille*. Artichokes, asparagus, and countless varieties of salad are also common.

Specialities to try

The most famous Provençal dishes are the bean-and-vegetable *pistou* soup, and saffron-flavoured *bouillabaisse* fish soup. Sea urchins are popular in Cassis, with the local wine of the same name. Lamb is also popular in Provence, as is *daube* (beef stewed in red wine) and *lapin à la provençale* (rabbit stewed in white wine, garlic, and mustard).

In the Languedoc, you'll find *tian* (a vegetable and rice gratin), *cassoulet* (beans and pork stewed in goose fat), *mourtayol* (chicken stew with saffron), mussels, and

BELOW *Roussillon's Mas Deu makes characterful wines that complement the strongly flavoured Catalan cuisine.*

ABOVE *This giant amphora on a roundabout in Narbonne is a reminder of the town's Roman heritage.*

RIGHT *Long avenues of plane trees offer welcome shade when driving or cycling.*

oysters from the Bassin de Thau (best accompanied with a bottle of Picpoul de Pinet), *cargolade* (snails grilled over vine stumps), and *langouste à la sètoise* (langoustines in a tomato, garlic, and cognac sauce).

In Roussillon, Catalan favourites include *pa amb tomaquets* (grilled bread with garlic and tomato), *escalivade* (grilled peppers in olive oil), *gambas à la planxa* (grilled prawns), *conill amb pebrots* (rabbit stew with peppers), *ollada* (pork and beans soup), and *boles de picolat* (meat stew in a green olive sauce). Anchovies also feature in Roussillon's cuisine, as the old fishing village of Collioure is the capital of the trade. *Tapenade* is a popular starter made from puréed olives and anchovies.

Say "cheese"

Provence isn't famous for its cheeses, though *banon* is a local favourite (a nutty cheese wrapped in chestnut leaves and made from goat's, sheep's, or cow's milk), as is *tomme arlésienne* (a creamy sheep's cheese with thyme and bay leaves). In the Languedoc, *pelardons* is a goat's cheese from the Cévennes. Roussillon also produces goat's and sheep's cheese. Sweet dessert wines commonly accompany cheeses. Chocolate cakes, fruit tarts, and ice-creams are popular desserts.

Roussillon has its own specialities like *bras de gitan* (a rolled, cream-filled cake) and *crème catalane* (a cinnamon-flavoured version of *crème brûlée*).

How to get there and get around

It's always a pleasure to fly to the south of France, especially if you're travelling from less sunny parts. As you step out of the plane in Nice, Montpellier or Perpignan, the warm air envelops you, the bright sunshine makes you squint, and the vivid colours astonish you. Even before you land, there's the thrill of seeing the Alps when flying into Nice, or the Pyrénées when touching down at Roussillon's tiny Perpignan-Rivesaltes airport. It's surrounded by vineyards and you have the impression of landing amid the vines themselves.

Arriving from the UK

Flying is increasingly the least expensive way to travel to the south of France from the UK, and a number of low-cost airlines – like EasyJet, Ryanair, and Openjet – operate direct, daily flights from London airports to Perpignan, Carcassonne, Nîmes, Montpellier, and Nice.

Flight times are generally under two hours and tickets can be purchased on-line. The cheapest tickets are available to those who book early on Ryanair from London to Perpignan. The major airlines – British Airways, Air France, British Midland – also offer competitive rates to airports here; Marseille tends to be the most expensive choice of destination.

The Eurostar from London allows you to connect with high-speed TGV rail links in Paris to destinations across the south. Journey time on Eurostar from London to Gare du Nord, Paris, via the Channel Tunnel is two and a half hours. You'll need to cross the city to the Gare de Lyon for connections to the south. From Paris, the TGV takes three hours to Marseille and around five to Perpignan.

In the summer, Eurostar runs a once-weekly service direct from London to Avignon, taking just over six hours. With prices typically not as competitive as the low-cost airlines, it doesn't always make sense to take the train and journey times can be considerably longer, but check www.sncf.com for more details.

There are no internal low-cost French airlines. And flying Air France from Paris to Perpignan, for example, can start to stretch your budget.

ABOVE *You can cycle around the Bassin de Thau, one of the Languedoc's biggest salt lakes, west of Montpellier, visiting ancient fishing villages on the way.*

RIGHT *Hiring a boat in Le Somail and visiting vineyards beside the Canal du Midi in the Minervois is an attractive option.*

The Channel Tunnel and ferries from the UK give you the option of bringing your own transport to France. The drive from Calais or Le Havre to the south takes around twelve hours non-stop, so you may want to break up the journey and spend a night en route.

Arriving from further away

If you're arriving in France from a long-haul destination such as the USA, you'll probably be flying into Paris Charles de Gaulle airport. To fly to the south, take the shuttle bus to Paris Orly airport and continue on an Air France flight from there.

Alternatively, there are trains from Charles de Gaulle airport to central Paris, and from the Gare de Lyon you can catch the TGV to stations in Roussillon, Languedoc, and Provence.

Renting a car

If you're not travelling with your car, don't expect to rely on public transport to get around the vineyards. Although the region's local trains and buses are efficient, regular services are limited to journeys between main towns, while journeys between the villages where most domaines are located are infrequent. Instead, consider renting a car from Budget, Hertz, Avis, Europcar, or the good value Sixt.

It is sensible to consider getting a vehicle with air conditioning in summer months – a convertible might sound like a good idea, but you'll fry in an open-top car in the summer.

Save this option for spring or autumn. For maps, try the Institut Géographique National series (*see* box p.30).

Tips for drivers

Driving around the south can be enormously pleasurable, especially if you stick to the quieter country roads. However, there are a few points to remember. First, people tend to drive fast and recklessly, so if someone's on your tail, pull over and let them pass. Second, the authorities take drink-driving seriously and the legal limit is stricter than in many other countries. Third, the French haven't phased out the hazardous practice of giving priority to cars joining a main road from the right and it's still a cause of many accidents. Fourth, the road traffic mortality rate in France is around double that in the UK. Fifth, speeding tickets are expensive and payable on the spot. Finally, the French have the commendable habit of alerting others to a police presence by flashing their headlights; you're not expected to flash back.

Cycling – the pleasures and perils

Cycling can be fun, particularly around some of the smaller appellations like Palette or Bellet in Provence. The best advice is to look at the maps and decide, based on your fitness level and proficiency, if cycling is an option for you. If you take a bike, you'll mostly be exploring small country lanes where the châteaux and domaines are located. Avoid busy main roads and take plenty of water to drink. Take spare parts, too, if your bike's specifications are imperial rather than metric.

There's a commonly held belief that France is a nation of cyclists and that drivers are courteous to them. This *risky* assumption stems from the French hosting the Tour de France cycling competition. In fact, about half of all admissions to accident and emergency wards in the summer in the south are cyclists. Part of the problem is the number of foreign drivers on the roads, so if you're going to be one of those drivers, spare a thought for the cyclist.

Finally, canal boats offer a leisurely way to see parts of the south, and this option is discussed where appropriate in Part Two.

Where to stay

Recommendations about where to stay in each wine region in the south of France feature in this guide. Accommodation options include an attractive villa bed and breakfast overlooking Nice, an historic wine château in the Côtes de Provence, a grand hotel near the amphitheatre in Nîmes, an authentic *vigneron*'s house in a Corbières village, and a classy hotel in Perpignan's medieval quarter. Some recommendations place you in the centre of a town, others put you amid the vines, but all have been selected for their character and friendliness. Additionally, accommodation options are proposed with a variety of budgets in mind.

RIGHT *Limoux hosts the longest carnival in the Languedoc: it runs from January to March.*

BELOW *No matter what time of year you visit, the south of France is always in bloom.*

Check out these websites

There are also several useful tourism companies in France with websites that allow you to search for accommodation by region, price, and facilities. For luxury accommodation, check out Châteaux & Hotels de France (www.chateauxhotels.com); this allows you to select accommodation according to activity, including wine tourism. Hotel en Europe (www.express-hotel.net) is a portal to various hotel reservation agencies and by clicking on "France" you can select your destination city and choose from a number of accommodation providers.

The French railway company SNCF also has an excellent website (www.voyages-sncf.com) that also allows you to search for hotel accommodation by city. Alternatively, the Logis de France group (www.logis-de-france.fr) represents a wide variety of privately owned, independent hotels under the slogan "hotels with a human face". It doesn't represent hotel or motel chains, so you're likely to find accommodation with an authentic, local character.

Chain gangs

There are a number of inexpensive and comfortable motel and hotel chains in France that provide reliable and decent accommodation. They're also easy to find, as they're well signposted and located on the outskirts of major towns and cities. They include the ultra-low-cost Formule 1 motel chain (www.hotelformule1.com), whose simple rooms make up in convenience and cleanliness what they lack in charm. The Etap motel chain (www.etaphotel.com) offers a similar deal. Neither have restaurants but usually there's a choice of eateries in the immediate vicinity. Cheap hotel-restaurant chains include Campanile (www.campanile.fr) and the affordably superior Ibis group (www.ibishotel.com). Again, these hotels are well signposted and typically located at the entrance to any major town or city.

The rental option

Of course, you may prefer to rent accommodation if you're staying for a week or longer in one place. The Gîtes de France website (www.gites-de-france.fr) allows you to choose from different accommodation options by region and to book online. Alternatively, check the classified advertisements in your newspaper's travel section. Camping is also an attractive, relatively inexpensive option for longer stays. The weather is likely to be kind and the facilities can be on a par with those of a decent hotel (swimming pool, bars, restaurants, and so on). Most campsites are also happy to cater for campervans.

Travelling around

In addition to accommodation recommendations, this guide proposes itineraries: each chapter identifies wine towns and villages of interest, as well as producers to visit, with full contact details, while the accompanying maps provide a visual orientation to the regions. Although many domaines are signposted, the green Institut Géographique National maps are also helpful (see box p.30). The itineraries point you in the right direction rather than dictate where you should turn left or right. They therefore allow you the flexibility to devise your own trip and so choose which routes best fit in with your schedule and means of transport.

The winemakers

I f there's one attribute shared by the people who make the wines described in this guide, it's passion. The word crops up repeatedly in conversations with *vignerons* and one has the strong impression that what they're doing is not just a job – it's a vocation, a genuine calling. Significantly, this sentiment is frequently accompanied by a palpable optimism and a pioneering sense that the south of France is truly the New World of French winemaking.

FINDING THE VINEYARDS

Getting around the south of France's vineyards is always **great fun** and often an **adventure**. Fortunately, many of the wine estates featured in this guide are well signposted and local **tourist offices can often provide wine maps** for tourists. Inevitably though, when you're trying to find a château or domaine, you'll head up the wrong track, **take a wrong turn**, **get completely lost and then discover some wonderful, hidden estate** that doesn't feature in this book. So hang onto your sense of humour, **keep your eyes open** and give yourself lots of time. And take some good road maps with you. Available at all good French bookshops **the green Institut Géographique National maps** are particularly useful and feature many of the domaines in this guide (albeit in tiny print) – buy numbers 72 (Roussillon), 65 and 66 (Languedoc), plus 67 and 68 (Provence).

RIGHT *Château de Jau, one of the largest family properties in Roussillon, covers an impressive 135ha.*

Spurs to success

A spirit of innovation and experimentation infects even those with long experience of winemaking. Why? Because in the last twenty-five years, with the widespread introduction of new winemaking technologies, the possibility of making good wines has captured their imagination. Of course, competition from all quarters of the winemaking world – and the recognition that mediocre wines have no market – have also been spurs.

New domaines appear each year. Some are created from scratch. Others are old estates now bottling their own wines, rather than taking their grapes to the local cooperative. Meanwhile, cooperatives have also invested heavily. One of their main challenges today is to entice their members to improve the quality of their grapes. The days of settling simply for quantity are over.

The role of cooperatives

As you travel around the wine regions and visit the independent producers featured in this guide, it's hard to overlook the significant role that cooperatives still play. The largest building in most villages in the region is still the local co-op, and you can usually find it located at the entrance to the village. Many of these date from the earliest days of the cooperative movement and bear names expressive of the aspirations of their founders – like the l'Indispensable and the l'Amicale in Provence, or the Les Vignerons Libres co-op in the Languedoc.

How the cooperatives started

The cooperative movement began in the Languedoc department of the Hérault in 1901. Many *vignerons* at that time saw *caves coopératives* as a way for small producers collectively to compete with large estates and to negotiate better deals with the powerful wine merchants or *négociants*. Négociants had risen to prominence in the south's wine economy during the first half of the nineteenth century with the advent of industrialization, and they continue to play an important role today. For example, négociants can find export markets for small producers and can create brands to sell their wines.

By 1914, around eighty cooperatives were spread across the south. Initially they just helped to sell the wines that *vignerons* themselves produced. Later, co-ops began to vinify their members' grapes and bottle wines as well. A boom in the cooperative movement occurred during the inter-war years when around 750 new co-ops were founded. The expansion in the movement coincided with a significant increase in French wine consumption. Today, many co-ops belong to larger associations called *groupements de producteurs* that focus on the large-scale supermarket trade. The most famous of these are the Vignerons du Val d'Orbieu in the Languedoc and the Vignerons Catalans in Roussillon.

Size makes the difference

The difference between cooperative members and independent growers is that co-op members tend to be small-scale family enterprises with holdings of often less than three hectares (ha) – at which size bottling your own wine might not be feasible. By contrast, the smallest independent domaines – the *caves particulières* – tend to be around 10ha. The largest may have vineyards of 150ha, and the entire estate may be as much as 300ha.

A CO-OP TO LOOK OUT FOR

Some cooperatives, like the **Producteurs de Mont Tauch** in Fitou, promote the wines from individual members' vineyards, and these *vignerons'* names and faces feature on the bottles. The Mont Tauch cooperative has also **identified the specific characteristic of each of its members' vineyard plots** with a view to improving the selection of grapes. This has been a mammoth task involving the inspection of **thousands of plots, some of which are tiny and isolated.**

It's not difficult to understand why winemakers here should feel **passionate about their vocation.** They live in a beautiful part of the world blessed by a good climate. **Their vines generally produce ripe, healthy, and concentrated grapes.** Nevertheless, while it's common to hear a *vigneron* speak about his or her "passion", they would never admit that they're satisfied. **The desire to do even better is ever present.**

How wine is made

French wines are made according to appellation regulations that govern what grapes you can grow, where you can grow them, how you should harvest, vinify, and age them, and how you can label the finished product. In short, *appellation contrôlée* (AC) rules rule. With their love of classification and bureaucracy, it's not surprising that the French have the most extensive and sophisticated AC system in the world. There's even an appellation for hay, from Arles, plus ACs for almost every other conceivable agricultural product, like rice, salt, olive oil, butter, vinegar, honey, and nuts.

INAO: the boss of wine

The government body authorized to supervise these regulations is the Institut National des Appellations d'Origine (INAO), which was established in 1934. The INAO's wine committee is made up of government-appointed wine professionals who consider their role to be that of guardians of France's wine heritage. Their decisions may not be modified under any circumstances, either by government or by any other authority.

The AC argument

Not everyone in the quickly evolving wine scene here is a fan of the appellation system. Those who want the freedom to make fine wines from unorthodox grape varieties using methods unacceptable to the authorities are particularly vocal in their criticism. A few such *vignerons* simply make whatever wines

they want to, even if the final product only qualifies for the humble *vin de table* status. Their main complaint is that the system is too rigid and too slow to evolve. They argue that appellation rules should be more flexible towards innovations that improve quality. They also argue that the rules should respond faster to market demands. Not surprisingly, there are quite a few *vignerons* who flout the regulations.

Supporters of the system, on the other hand, argue that it ensures the continuity of tradition and gets a higher price for their wines. They argue that too much flexibility in the system risks diluting what makes a region special.

Industry versus craft

The debate over how wines should be made in the south came to a head back in 2001 when the Californian winemaker Robert Mondavi was denied permission to make wine his way in the Languedoc. Mondavi wanted to raze a 50ha area of wooded hillside, a plan which raised environmentalists' eyebrows, and plant a vineyard.

Led by the newly installed mayor, cult winemaker Aimé Guibert (see Domaine Mas de Daumas Gassac, p.92), the local council of Aniane, a village north of Montpellier, rejected Mondavi's plans following a twelve-month row after his proposals had initially been endorsed by the previous council. The intervening council elections were virtually fought over this one issue. It was Guibert's objections to "computerized winemaking" and "industrial wines" with "no soul, no poetry" that had got him elected in the first place.

The role of technology

The south of France's wines couldn't have got where they are today without inventions such as de-stemming machines, pneumatic presses, refrigerated stainless-steel vats, carbonic maceration, and, increasingly, micro-oxygenation. However, the technology didn't create the current wine culture (Guibert's objection to "Californisation") – instead, the existing wine culture learned to apply the new technology to the task of improving traditional wines.

ABOVE *This old wine press, at Domaine de l'Hospitalet, east of Narbonne, is purely for show.*

LEFT *Oak aging takes place in an ultra-modern cellar at Château Puech-Haut in the Grès de Montpellier.*

ABOVE *Winemaking in Malepère is dominated by cooperatives, like this well-equipped one in Arzens.*

RIGHT *Pictures adorn the walls at the Miquel family's tasting room at Château Cazal-Viel in St-Chinian's Orb Valley.*

In the vineyard

"Great wines", you'll hear, "are made in the vineyard" and the last twenty years or so have also seen many developments in the vineyards. For example, it's not uncommon these days to meet a *vigneron* who practises "green" viticulture (*see* box p.14). Techniques are being used to limit yields. New vineyards are planted more densely than previously, as this yields fruit with greater concentration. And more attention than before is given to the location of vineyards, with the trend away from coastal areas in favour of hillside locations.

So have these developments made a difference? And is it possible for a novice to distinguish a well-made wine from a stinker? There's little debate over the first question. Countless visitors and wine professionals alike have noticed the improvement in quality. However, you may still encounter the complacent *vigneron* who's happy to sell to the passing tourist trade and has little concern with quality.

How to spot good growers

To detect these wines and avoid them, look first at the domaine's vineyards. Unruly, overgrown vines suggest low yields are not important. Try to find out if the domaine has planted any *cépages améliorateurs* ("better grapes", in other words) like Cabernet Sauvignon, Syrah or Mourvèdre for reds and Marsanne, Roussanne or Rolle for whites. Then look at the *cave*. Hygiene is important, but don't be alarmed by concrete or fibreglass vats; they're just as effective as any other type of container. Look for oak barrels, too. Their presence may indicate that the domaine's wines are worthy of ageing.

Then look at the wine. An inferior one will give itself away by appearing dull, which means it's been ove-filtered, fined or pumped around – bruising treatments that the best *vignerons* minimize. Finally, how does the wine smell and taste? Do you like it? Does it have an attractive, long finish? In the final analysis, what counts is whether it pleases you. And if it's inexpensive, so much the better. Be adventurous. There are hundreds of *vignerons* out there. You'll find discovering wine country off the beaten track is always a rewarding adventure. You may even stumble across the next cult winemaker.

The etiquette of visiting winemakers

Visiting a domaine or a cooperative and talking to the winemaker is a great way to buy wine and learn about it. It's much more fun than going to the supermarket. It's also much more intimate. *Vignerons* are passionate about their wines and keen to share their enthusiasm. Many of the domaines featured in this guide are small family affairs with few, if any, permanent staff. Others are large family businesses with purpose-built tasting rooms and boutiques full of local products. You may be the only ones visiting a smaller domaine, but in recent years even the smallest domaines have become open to the idea of *tourisme et vignoble* and visitors are warmly welcomed. Larger estates are often more organized about receiving visitors, even groups, but the welcome is no less warm.

Some conversational gambits

When you meet the *vigneron* or a member of staff, you'll probably want to ask about the domaine's history. This is a good way to receive an introduction to the domaine. Ask about terroir (the vineyard's characteristics), *encépagement* (the mix of grape varieties), *rendements* (the yields), vinification (how the wine was made), *élevage* (how the wine was matured), and *millésime* (what the year was like), and you'll soon be hearing all about the *vigneron's* approach. Being French, this will quickly turn philosophical, poetical and finally quasi-mystical, but don't worry; this just means your host is happy to see you.

Things you must do

First, telephone ahead where indicated to make sure there will be someone there. This is a courtesy, but can also save you a wasted journey.

Make small talk on arriving. *"Il fait beau"* ("the weather is fine") is usually applicable, followed by *"il fait du vent"* ("it's windy") — as it will be one day in three. The wind will be the Mistral, Cers or Tramontane, depending on whether you're in Provence, Languedoc or Roussillon.

Show the *vigneron* this book — to show you're genuinely interested — and explain what you'd like to taste, either *"la gamme"* ("the range") or a

ABOVE *Many domaines are well signposted, but others are hidden and off the beaten track.*

RIGHT *The Vietnamese Buddhist Hong Hien Pagoda outside Frèjus is a reminder of France's colonial past.*

part of it, like the reds, the rosés, or the whites. Look around while the glasses are being arranged and make an appreciative remark like *"c'est sympa"* ("it's appealing, friendly").

Contemplate the wine in your glass, tilt the glass towards the light and say *"belle robe"* ("nice frock" – meaning you like the colour). Then swirl the wine around (keeping it in the glass), plunge your nose in, sniff audibly, contemplate for a moment and say *"c'est très fruité"* or *"floral"* or *"complexe"* if you can't decide.

Ask for *"le crachoir"* (a spittoon) so you can spit out what you don't want and empty what's left in your glass before the next wine. This minimizes the risk of getting inebriated. Take a big sip, slosh it around in your mouth, draw air in audibly, swallow or spit and say *"bien charpenté"* ("well structured") or *"très élégant"* ("very elegant") or *"belle longueur"* if the taste persists attractively.

Then ask to see *"le tarif"* (the price list) and buy something, even if it's only some local honey. If you don't want to buy, offer to pay for what you've tasted (this will be declined), or ask where the wines are available at home and make a note.

Things you must not do
Don't arrive the worse for wear and don't drive over the family dog. Never arrive during lunch (or even the post-lunch siesta, which gets longer and later the closer you are to Spain). It's best to give small domaines a wide berth between noon and 3pm. By the same measure don't arrive too late in the evening, like after 7.30pm.

When you arrive, don't be afraid to knock on doors and ring bells. One producer has a doorbell like a claxon that he can hear in the vineyard. Don't decline an invitation to visit the vineyard or see the bottling line (okay, maybe you could refuse the latter, especially if it's your third in a week).

Never say that you don't like the wine – instead say that it's *"intéressant"* ("interesting") or has *"caractère"* ("character"); these can be compliments too. Don't worry if you can't find words to describe the wine; your host will almost certainly chip in, and you can simply nod. Finally, remember never to tip.

Time out from wine

There's a lot to do, buy, and see in the south of France while taking a break from discovering the wine country. There are world-class museums in Nice, fascinating markets in Aix-en-Provence, Roman amphitheatres in Arles and Nîmes, theatres and festivals in Montpellier and Perpignan, plus long stretches of sandy beaches from the Côte d'Azur to the Côte Vermeille. Each region has its own traditional crafts and contemporary artists, with galleries and gift shops galore.

The attractions of Nice

If you're staying in Nice, a lively carnival takes place during the two weeks before Lent and there's an international jazz festival in the third week of August. Nice also has excellent galleries dedicated to the works of former residents Matisse and Chagal. Less well-known is the beautiful and austere white marble Musée des Arts Asiatiques. But, Nice is also famous for its markets and shopping. Vieux Nice, located east of Place Massena, is the trendiest part of town with boutiques, bistros, and cafés. The port area around Rue Antoine-Gauthier and the Village Ségurane are two of the best places to buy antiques in the south.

The perched village of Eze, just east of Nice towards Monte-Carlo, is worth a detour. On the way back, visit the Villa Ephrussi at St-Jean-Cap-Ferrat, the fantasy house of flamboyant Béatrice de Rothschild. The Italianate villa is full of art treasures, while Provençal, English, Japanese, and Spanish gardens provide spectacular views towards the harbour at Villefranche.

The coast road to Frèjus, west of Nice, is one of the prettiest and takes in lively Antibes and Cannes, the film festival and shopping capital. The Musée Picasso in Antibes is worth a visit – Picasso used the château as a studio after World War II. The road leading from Cannes to Frèjus follows the stunning Corniche de l'Esterel, where the red massif plunges into the Mediterranean.

A trip to St-Tropez

Frèjus is a market town and naval base founded by the Romans. The medieval Cité Episcopale – with its cathedral, bishop's palace, baptistery, chapterhouse, cloisters, and archaeological museum – is worth visiting. It's a short trip from Frèjus to the pretty port of St-Tropez and its celebrated beaches: Tahiti, Pampelonne, and l'Escalet. Outside the midsummer tourist period it's a delightful place to visit and shop. You might never wear

them, but St-Tropez is the place to buy gladiator-style espadrilles called *sandals tropéziennes*. Alternatively, take home some Provençal fabrics or designer clothes. Pipe smokers should visit Courrieu Pipes, the oldest briar-pipe manufacturer in France, in nearby Cogolin. The town is also celebrated for its Armenian rugs.

The coastal Corniche des Maures is the last leg of the Côte d'Azur. It ends with the swanky châteaux along the Cap de Brégançon peninsula and lovely Hyères with its old town, parks, and villas. The cubist Villa de Noailles in Hyères, designed by architect Robert Mallet-Stevens, is worth a visit. However, give the nearby naval town of Toulon a wide berth. Apart from being ugly, it is the heartland of France's xenophobic National Front.

Where the Marseillais lose their money

The towns of Bandol and Cassis are pretty and fashionable ports between Toulon and Marseille. Windsurfing, diving, and canoeing are popular sports along this part of the coastline, especially around the *calanques* (mini-fjords) west of Cassis. Meanwhile the casinos in Bandol and Cassis attract gamblers from Marseille.

When they're not at the gaming tables, the brash Marseillais are probably shopping along the rue St-Ferréol, the city's main commercial district. If you're visiting Marseille, a good plan is to take the three-hour bilingual Histobus bus tour run by RTM (Réseau de Transport Marseillais) from the old port (2pm daily July to September; Sunday only out of season). It will give you a feel for the layout of the city.

ABOVE *Smokers will want to buy a handcrafted briar from Courrieu, pipe-makers in Cogolin, Provence.*

BELOW *Colourful pottery like this in Collioure, Roussillon, is found all over the south.*

The pleasures of Aix

North of Marseille is beautiful Aix-en-Provence, the place to buy local pottery, *calissons* (almond and glazed melon sweets), and olive oil. It's also famous for its International Opera Festival in July – one of the city's numerous summer music and arts festivals. Aix boasts the most delightful markets (Tuesdays, Thursdays, and Saturdays) and one of the prettiest streets in Provence, the Cours Mirabeau, with its fine seventeenth- and eighteenth-century *hôtels particulières*, or private houses.

Nostradamus' home town

Salon-de-Provence, west of Aix, is another place to buy Provence's finest olive oils; it's also home to the *savon de Marseille* (Marseille soap) industry. Place Crousillat, with its moss-covered fountain, is the prettiest square in Salon. It's just outside the walled Old Town, which is accessed via the seventeenth-century Tour de l'Horloge. The centre of the gentrified old quarter is Place de l'Ancienne Halle, a large square from which rue de Nostradamus leads to the philosopher-astrologer's house. The Château-Musée de l'Emperi, one of Provence's oldest remaining castles, is also just off the square.

Roman remains in Arles and Nîmes

Arles, directly west of Salon on the Rhône, is famous for a magnificent Roman amphitheatre, its links with Vincent van Gogh, and gypsy music. It has several fine museums, like the Muséon Arlaten, established by Provence's poet laureate, Frédéric Mistral, which records daily Provençal life in the past. The Musée de l'Arles Antique tells the story of Roman Arles, with fine architectural models.

Fans of birdwatching should head south to the Camargue wetlands to check out the flamingos. But, supporters of animal rights will want to avoid Arles during the Féria de Pâques at Easter when bullfights take place in the amphitheatre.

Bullfights also feature in Nîmes, to the west of Arles. Its amphitheatre is the best preserved of any surviving Roman arena and the nearby Maison Carrée is the world's best-preserved Roman temple. It stands opposite the modernist Carrée d'Art, designed by Norman Foster and containing the city's Musée d'Art Contemporain. Nîmes' fine old mansions make strolling around the Old Town a delight.

North of Nîmes is the superb Roman aqueduct, the Pont du Gard. Nearby is perfectly restored Uzès, dominated by the twelfth-century castle of the Duché – the first dukes of France. To the south, there's the medieval walled town of Aigues-Mortes from where the saint-king Louis IX embarked on his crusades to Cyprus and Tunis.

DON'T MISS THE MARKETS

Wherever you are, you'll want to visit a market. From Nice to Perpignan, **stalls are overflowing** with an abundance of mouth-watering fruits and vegetables, herbs and spices, country breads, and **stacks of cheeses** plus seafood and charcuterie, and an array of regional wines. Incredibly, even the smallest towns stage a lively market twice a week.

You can have a picnic tasting olive oils drizzled on fresh bread, nibbling artisanal cheeses, and sipping wine at a *vigneron*'s stall. **There's no obligation to buy, but you'll find it hard to resist.** When you're done, there'll be a café nearby to **refresh yourself with an aniseed-flavoured pastis**, a favourite local tipple.

ABOVE *Bullfighting festivals are common in the south.*

RIGHT *Before the advent of bottling, some estates only sold wine from the barrel.*

ABOVE RIGHT *Supermarkets feature regional wines, though buying direct from the producer costs the same and is more fun.*

Montpellier – the capital of Languedoc

West of Aigues-Mortes is the vibrant university city of Montpellier, the capital of Languedoc. The city's calendar is packed with festivals and artistic events. Its main shopping and café life is around the splendid place de la Comédie, off which streets lead to the city's medieval quarter in one direction and to the modernist Triangle, Polygon, and Antigone quarters in the other. The nearby Corum houses the city's theatres, opera hall, and exhibition centre.

Montpellier also boasts the oldest botanical garden in France, the Jardin des Plantes. It's not far from another Montpellier landmark, the Château d'Eau, a neoclassical temple at one end of the Promenade du Peyrou, an attractive park west of the place de la Comédie. The place de la Canourgue is the best place in town to shop for antiques.

Gothic Narbonne

As you follow the coast towards Perpignan, you pass through the somewhat neglected town of Béziers and the much more agreeable Roman town of Narbonne. Narbonne boasts possibly the finest gothic cathedral in the south of France. Alongside it is a section of the Via Domitia, the Roman route to Spain. With its medieval monuments, its grand Hôtel de Ville and excellent museums, Narbonne feels like a big city. Its lively shopping streets are behind the café-fronted boulevards on either side of the pretty Canal de la Robine in the town centre.

Cosmopolitan Perpignan

An hour and a half's drive south and you're in France's sunniest and most cosmopolitan city, Perpignan. The thirteenth-century palace of the kings of Majorca, who ruled here for 100 years, dominates the place. Beneath its ramparts is the medieval quarter with lively market squares, cafés and shopping streets. The gothic masterpiece, the Loge de Mer, next to the Hôtel de Ville in the Old Town, houses one of the city's smartest cafés. In July and August there's a street festival every Thursday evening.

Perpignan's most distinctive landmark, the Castillet, a fourteenth-century gate, is beside a pleasant canal moat, La Basse, bordered with flowerbeds and cafés.

How to get your wine home

The temptation to buy wine to take home is enormous. Apart from the fact that it can be extremely good value for money, you'll probably want to take certain wines home because they're simply not available there. You might also want to take wines home to prolong that feeling of being on holiday. Remember though: a crisp, dry Provençal rosé just doesn't taste the same on a cloudy northern afternoon as it does on a sunny terrace in St-Tropez – so buy what you're sure you'll enjoy back home.

The practicalities

Unless you're travelling by car, the chances are you'll be limited by the size of aircraft overhead lockers – and by what you can carry. In other words, half a case or a ten-litre bag-in-box. There's the option of posting your purchases (although some restrictions apply, for example to North America, so check your country's rules). Unfortunately, few *vignerons* offer a postage and packing service, so it'll be up to you to organize this.

To make matters worse, it's actually hard in France to find suitable cartons for posting wine. Some large French DIY shops stock padded wine cases, but these are not widely available at La Poste ("the post office"). One option is to buy purpose-made, single-bottle padded cartons (available in the UK from main Post Office branches) before you leave. Of course, the price of postage and packing – whether of a case or a single bottle – may cost more than the wine itself, so this is not necessarily an economical option.

CUSTOMS RULES

There are few restrictions for Europeans on the quantity that can be taken home. For example, the UK government states that you can bring as much wine back as you like – **provided that it's for personal consumption**. The UK government's "indicative level" is ninety litres of wine – what the government believes a normal person might consume in six months. Over this, you might have to **persuade customs officers** that you're not a smuggler. Or, perhaps, that you're having a lot of parties. For **advice on allowances**, contact HM Customs and Excise National Advice Service (0845 010 9000, www.hmce.gov.uk).

Discovering Vineyards in the South of France

Provence

Nice and Bellet

N ice's best-kept secret, apart from excellent ravioli (this is where it was invented), is the tiny and exclusive appellation of Bellet. It's tucked away in the hills amid swanky villas and greenhouses of carnations less than thirty minutes from the celebrated, palm-lined Promenade des Anglais. There is just a handful of producers, and you can visit them all in a day. They're dotted between the villages of St-Isidore and St-Roman-de-Bellet, within the city's limits. Bellet owes its fame to a crisp, dry white wine based on the increasingly fashionable Rolle grape, once found only here and in Corsica.

Nice's best-kept secret

The Niçois have jealously kept Bellet wines to themselves for at least three centuries, and they're still hard to find outside the city's limits. They rarely get further than the cellars of Nice's top restaurants like the *belle epoque* Le Chantecler at the Hotel Négresco, where they're the favourite accompaniment to local specialities like sea bass and *bourride*, a tasty fish soup.

The vineyards were more extensive in 1860 when Nice and the rest of the Alpes-Maritimes became part of France. In the early twentieth century, after the phylloxera blight, many vineyards were turned over to market gardening and flowers. Today, they're standing their ground against the encroachment of yet more villas and greenhouses. In fact, Bellet happens to be the only appellation in France located within the boundaries of a city and it's unlikely to expand beyond its current 60ha. Some producers make fewer than 2,000 bottles a year.

Bellet was created in 1941, making it one of the oldest appellations in France. It

LOCAL INFORMATION

Office de Tourisme
SNCF Gare Nice Ville
Tel: 08 92 70 74 07
info@nicetourism.com
www.nicetourism.com

JML bike hire
34 ave Auber, 06000 Nice
Tel: 04 93 16 07 00

Rent-a-Car
ave Thiers, 06000 Nice
Tel: 04 93 88 69 69

BUSES: **Gare Routière**
Blvd Jean Jaurès, 06000 Nice
Tel: 04 93 85 61 81

TRAINS: **Nice CP Gare du Sud**
Tel: 04 97 03 80 80
www.trainprovence.com

came of age in the 1960s after some teething troubles, including narrowly avoiding demotion two years after gaining AC status. Château de Bellet, owned by the president of the *syndicat*, is probably the best-known producer and the unofficial guardian of the appellation's reputation.

What the wines are like

The vineyards are neatly planted between fig and olive trees on small parcels and narrow terraces or *restanques* at 200–400m (650–1,300 feet) in altitude. The land is steep and sun-soaked, with relatively abundant rain for the area. The grey mixture of sandstone, limestone, and pudding stones is prone to soil erosion so some *vignerons* grow wild grasses between the vines to reduce the risk. The vineyards are immediately east of the Var Valley where alternating currents of sea and mountain air prevent overheating and keep the grapes healthy.

Bellet comes in all three colours and some grape varieties are unique to the appellation. The indigenous Braque, for example, is a fragile grape that gives red and rosé wines of distinction, with characteristic rosewater aromas. It's often

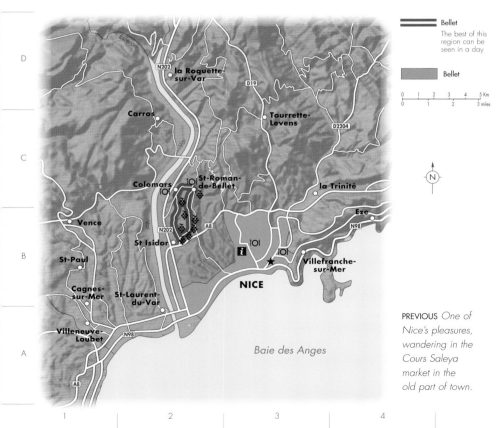

PREVIOUS *One of Nice's pleasures, wandering in the Cours Saleya market in the old part of town.*

blended with the dark-berried Folle Noire, another local variety and one famed for its capricious nature. Folle Noire gives candied fruit and peppery notes. Bellet reds are noble wines that can be aged for decades, if you can wait that long. If you can't, consult your bank manager and buy a 1990.

The rosés are made to accompany food and to be drunk young. They are *rosés de bouche* rather than apéritif-style *rosés de nez*. The famous Bellet whites are delicious young but age well. You'll find a drop of Chardonnay blended with the indigenous Rolle, giving floral and citrus aromas to these sought-after wines. The best are fermented and matured in oak. Bellet whites can be reminiscent of Chablis – especially oak-aged versions with a good dose of Chardonnay. They share a dry, crisp, nutty quality with Chablis and can age similarly well – over a decade in some cases.

Travelling around

If you're staying in Nice, visiting Bellet's vineyards couldn't be easier. Bus 62 from the Gare Routière goes to St-Roman-de-Bellet and takes in a good part of the Route des Vins. Alternatively, it's twelve minutes by train from the Gare du Sud to St-Isidore and services are frequent. You could combine the train and bicycle or take the car and walk. The wine route is just 15km (9 miles) long.

Begin your tour of Bellet's vineyards by heading west, away from Nice's city centre, to the nearby hamlet of St-Isidore. Start out in the square beneath the elegant church of St-Isidore (appropriately the patron saint of gardeners and protector of harvests) and follow the Chemin de Crémat to St-Roman-de-Bellet. The route takes in spectacular views of the surrounding Alpine peaks and nearly all of Bellet's producers. Wine tasting begins almost immediately as you'll shortly be at Domaine de Toasc and Domaine du Fogolar, where vineyards overlook the Var Valley.

Stay on the Chemin de Crémat for the magnificent Château de Crémat and pretty St-Roman-de-Bellet, where you can treat yourself (but not your wallet) to a meal at the friendly Auberge de Bellet. Head out of St-Roman-de-Bellet on the Chemin de Saquier to the beautiful Château de Bellet and, before heading back to Nice, spare time to enjoy the views from the Clot dóu Baile vineyards. Back in Nice, head for the city's best veggie restaurant, La Zucca Magica, or local institution Restaurant Lou Mourelec for affordable Niçoise fare.

Top growers in Nice and Bellet (*see also p.134*)

Château de Bellet

Les Séoules, 06200 Nice, tel: 04 93 37 81 57
This terracotta-coloured château with its twin towers and

(*see also p.134*)

GROWERS IN NICE AND BELLET

Domaine Augier
680 route de Bellet
06200 Nice
Tel: 04 93 37 81 47
Rose Augier makes characterful wines in her small basement cellar in St-Roman. Her white is particularly good.
(*B2: moderate*)

Domaine du Fogolar
370 chemin de Crémat
6200 Nice
Tel: 04 93 37 82 52
This is the most southerly domaine in Bellet and the place to buy a pure, barrel-fermented Rolle and red vins de garde. (*B2: moderate*)

Propriété Massa
425 chemin de Crémat
06200 Nice
Tel: 04 93 37 81 56
Jean Massa's traditional wines are handmade by an exacting personality and aged in chestnut barrels.
(*B2: moderate to expensive*)

Restanques de Bellon
rue Collet de Bellon
06200 Nice
Tel: 04 93 37 98 11
The domaine and studio of sculptor Sacha Sosnowski is the place to buy artistically-made white Bellet. (*B2: moderate*)

Domaine de Toasc
213 chemin de Crémat
06200 Nice
Tel: 04 92 15 14 14
Bernard Nicoletti is a rising star making his mark with an excellent Rolle-Chardonnay and a Braquet-Grenache rosé. (*B2: inexpensive to moderate*)

WHERE TO STAY AND EAT

Auberge de Bellet
629 Route de Bellet
06200 Nice
Tel: 04 93 37 83 84

Auberge du Redier
06670 Colomars
Tel: 04 92 15 19 00

Mme Michele Golle
69 Vieux Chemin de
Crémat
06200 Nice
Tel: 04 93 37 94 31

Hôtel Floride
52 Blvd de Cimiez
06000 Nice
Tel: 04 93 53 11 02

Restaurant Lou Mourelec
15 Rue Biscarra
06000 Nice
Tel: 04 93 80 80 11

La Zucca Magica
4 bis Quai Papacino
06000 Nice
Tel: 04 93 56 25 27

BELOW *An ancient window
in one of the many historic
buildings of the south.*

seventeenth-century chapel is set in parkland with views over the Var Valley and the Alps. It is arguably the appellation's driving force. Ghislain de Charnacé's family has been in Bellet for four centuries and de Charnace is president of the Bellet *syndicat*. He makes a pure Braquet rosé, plus long-lasting reds based on the grape and two excellent Rolle white *cuvées*. *(B2: expensive)*

Château Crémat
M. et Mme. Kamerbeek, 442 chemin de Crémat, 06200 Nice, tel: 04 92 15 12 15
An architectural marvel, built in the medieval "troubadour" style, that was fashionable at the start of the twentieth century, with its tower and crenellated walls. *(B2: moderate to expensive)*

Clot dóu Baile
277 chemin de Saquier, 06200 Nice, tel: 04 93 29 85 87
Louise Cambillau comes from a distinguished family of Algerian winemakers. In 1980, she and her husband bought land in Saquier, planted 6ha of *restanques* and built a cellar. Sadly, her husband died in 1990 and their son Ludovic died seven years later. Today, Ludovic's old friend Vincent Dauby is the winemaker and the domaine now covers 22ha. The reds are fruity, silky, and peppery; the rosés delicate and floral; the whites fresh and lemony with a hint of flint and green apples. Buy as much as you can. *(B2: moderate)*

Finding a place to stay
There are many accommodation options in Nice. The inexpensive, two-star Hôtel Floride in quiet Cimiez north of the centre near the Chagal museum has comfortable rooms and a garden. Another option is to stay near the wine domaines. Michele Golle offers bed and breakfast in a villa set in parkland with sea views and a swimming pool on the *route des vins*. Or try the elegant and gastronomic Auberge de Redier in Colomars just north of St-Roman-de-Bellet.

Other things to do
Nice is a lively city with fine museums, fabulous architecture and a fascinating old quarter. The daily market in the Cours Saleya in the *vieille ville* is a must-see. The Musée Matisse is nearby. You can buy a one-, three- or seven-day museum card (Carte Musées Côte d'Azur) for €8/15/25 from any museum.

Fans of vintage railways should head up the mountains on the scenic Train des Pignes to Digne-les-Bains (€34 for the round trip). There are four trains a day and the journey takes three and a quarter hours one-way (www.trainprovence.com). Alternatively, head for the sea for whale-watching from nearby Villefranche-sur-Mer (www.actiloisirs.com).

Côtes de Provence

This is a mammoth appellation, the largest in Provence, and France's principal rosé wine region. Sadly, few rosés leave the area as they're made to meet the demand for fun, easy-drinking and thirst-quenching wines among the Riviera's summer holiday crowds. And there's nothing better for sipping on the yacht than a cool, crisp, dry Provençal rosé. However, estates establishing reputations today are emphasizing Cabernet-based, oak-aged red *vins de garde* and characterful whites.

The classified growths of Côtes de Provence

An historical quirk means that the Côtes de Provence includes a number of classified estates, like Bordeaux. There are eighteen in all and sometimes the designation can be relied upon to identify a superior estate. These self-declared *cru classé* estates were officially recognized in 1955 but the system has never been extended. The appellation itself was recognized in 1977 and includes some 314 independent winemakers and forty-one cooperatives spread across the Var, the Bouches du Rhône and the Alpes Maritime. A staggering 110 million bottles are produced, eighty per cent of which are rosé.

What the wines are like

With such an array of terroirs, it's not surprising that there's no typical Côtes de Provence wine. In fact, the diversity of soils and microclimates means that the composition of vineyards can vary from one estate to the next. The whites, for example, from Ugni Blanc, Clairette, Sémillon, and Rolle, vary considerably from the north to the south of the appellation. The reds vary too, with Mourvèdre making up the blend on coastal estates and Syrah doing the job elsewhere. The rosés may include Cinsault and the delicate Tibouren too, depending where you are. Organic and biodynamic viticulture are much in evidence.

Some of the best wines come from Les Collines du Haut Pays, or the Hautes Côtes as they are called. This is back-country Provence, a long way from the palm trees and parasol pines of the coast. It is a landscape of perched villages and steep valleys. Half of all Côtes de Provence wines come from La Vallée Intérieure, where vineyards stretch out to the forests bordering the valley. Important wine towns are scattered across the landscape. The wines that benefit from the most generous climate come from La Bordure Maritime. These vineyards cover

GROWERS IN COTE DE PROVENCE

Château Bertaud-Belieu
83580 Gassin
Tel: 04 94 56 16 83
This estate's cave resembles
a Roman temple. Buy the
Cuvée Bélieu. (B2: moderate)

Château du Galoupet
St-Nicholas
83250 La Londe-les-Maures
Tel: 04 94 66 40 07
Cru classé estate with
luxurious flora, footpaths,
and panoramic views.
(B4: inexpensive)

Château Minuty
83580 Gassin
Tel: 04 94 56 12 09
A lovely cru classé estate
with a park, chapel, and an
eighteenth-century mas.
(B2: inexpensive to expensive)

Clos Mireille
route du Fort de Brégançon
83250 La Londe-les-Maures
Tel: 04 94 01 53 50
The Ott family specialize
in Bordeaux-style whites.
(B4: moderate to expensive)

Domaine de la Courtade
83400 Ile-de-Porquerolles
Tel: 04 94 58 31 44
This architecturally stylish
estate produces two cuvées.
(A4: moderate to expensive)

Domaine de la Tourre
Hameau de la Tourre
83310 Grimaud
Tel: 04 94 43 27 78
Look for Cuvée Charlemagne
at this rustic domaine.
(C2: inexpensive to moderate)

**Les Maîtres Vignerons de la
Presqu'Ile de St-Tropez**
La Foux, 83580 Gassin
Tel: 04 94 56 32 04
Buy the Château Pampelonne
or the popular Carte Noire.
(B2: inexpensive to moderate)

breathtaking scenery from the Estérel mountains around Fréjus and the Maures above St-Tropez to the most beautiful vineyards in France on the Ile de Porquerolles.

A region in five parts

Although this is a diverse and dispersed appellation, five distinct sub-regions can be identified: La Bordure Maritime – the coast from Fréjus to Hyères; La Vallée Intérieure – north of the Massif des Maures and south of the A8 between Toulon, Brignoles, and Le Muy; Les Collines du Haut Pays – the foothills north of the A8 between Brignoles and Les Arcs; Le Bassin du Beausset – between Bandol and Cassis (see p.56); and Ste-Victoire – west of the Coteaux Varois between St-Maximin and Aix-en-Provence (see p.60).

Travelling around

Count on spending at least three or four days exploring the Côtes de Provence wine country, and give yourself extra time to make it to the beautiful Ile de Porquorelles. The region divides into coastal routes and inland routes. If you're arriving from Marseille, you'll probably pass through Toulon, where you pick up the A57/A8 to join the inland routes and the A570/N98 to head for the coast – both roads head towards Frèjus, to the east of the appellation, and Nice. Alternatively, if you're arriving from Aix-en-Provence, follow the A8 (otherwise known as La Provençale) east. This route takes you through the inland vineyards and on to Frèjus.

Begin exploring the Côtes de Provence with producers north of historic Frèjus around the densely wooded Bagnols-en-Forêt (E2). Check out the astonishing red Mosque Missiri as you head north to Château de Cabran, an old fortified farm on the edge of Forêt Domaniale de Terres Gastes. Continue on up to the medieval hillside village of Bagnols-en-Forêt, then head west through the spectacular Gorges du Blavet and the Forêt du Rouët to beautiful Château du Rouët (D2). The route back to Frèjus follows the Argens Valley, between the Massif des Maures and the Estérel foothills, and takes in the sensational perched Domaine des Planes.

Next, head for the Hautes Côtes and La Vallée Intérieure, starting out at the splendid La Maison des Vins Côtes de Provence in Les Arcs. The appellation's showcase includes over 600 wines in a purpose-built cave de dégustation with adjoining gastronomic Provençal restaurant. From Les Arcs, head north via Château Ste-Roseline (D2) to the army town of Draguignan, Baron Haussmann's gateway to the Gorges du Verdon, with its compact medieval centre and palm-shaded boulevards. The route from Draguignan to Carcès takes in a number of producers including Domaine Ste-Croix. Fit in a visit to the Cistercian

Abbaye du Thoronet. Head south from Carcès, past the lake, through historic Cabasse to Pignans, at the foot of the Massif des Maures (a trip north from Carcès to Cotignan is worth a detour). The route from Pignans back to Les Arcs takes in Gonfaron, with its tortoise sanctuary, medieval Le Luc and pretty Taradeau, home to the Châteaux de Selle and de St-Martin.

The Bordure Maritime route includes producers around St-Tropez and Hyères in the south of the appellation. Take either the coastal N98 from Frèjus (beware the summer traffic) or the D25 from Le Muy (D2) through the Massif des Maures (sadly, this takes in the devastation caused by the September 2003 fires) to get there.

A good place to begin exploring the Golfe of St-Tropez's vineyards is the medieval village of Grimaud where Comaine de la Tourre is based (*C2*). There are great views from the ruined castle.

Côtes de Provence

Allow three to four days, plus extra for visiting the Ile de Porquerolles

GROWERS CONTINUED

Château de Cabran
83480 Puget-sur-Argens
Tel: 04 94 40 80 32 *(D1)*

Château Roubine
83510 Lorgues
Tel: 04 94 85 94 94 *(D3: moderate to expensive)*

Chateau du Rouët
83490 Le Muy
Tel: 04 94 99 21 10 *(D2)*

Château St-Baillon
83340 Flassans-sur-Issole
Tel: 04 94 69 74 60 *(D4)*

Château de St-Martin
83460 Taradeau
Tel: 04 94 99 76 76 *(D2)*

Château Ste-Roseline
83460 Les Arcs-sur-Argens
Tel: 04 94 99 50 30 *(D3)*

Commanderie de Peyrassol
83340 Flassans-sur-Issole
Tel: 04 94 69 74 60 *(D4: moderate to expensive)*

Domaine de l'Abbaye
83340 Le Thoronet
Tel: 04 94 73 87 36 *(D4)*

Domaine de la Bastide Neuve
83340 Le Cannet-des-Maures
Tel: 04 94 50 09 80 *(D3)*

Domaine des Planes
83520 Roquebrune-sur-Argens
Tel: 04 98 11 49 00 *(D2: inexpensive to moderate)*

Domaine de Rimauresq
83790 Pignans
Tel: 04 94 48 80 45 *(C4)*

Domaine Ste-Croix
83570 Carcès
Tel: 04 94 04 56 51 *(D4)*

PRICES: moderate (other than where specified)

Nearby Cogolin, with its winery Château St-Maur, Gassin with Châteaux Minuty and Bertaud-Belieu, and Ramatuelle are some of the prettiest hilltop villages anywhere. Further west, discover some of the sensational coastal domaines between colourful Bourmes-les-Mimosas and Hyères, like Château de Brégançon on the exclusive Brégançon peninsula *(B4)*. Ferries from La Tour Fondue take you to the Ile de Porquerolles where a bicycle is the best way to get around (visitor numbers are limited by quota so book your crossing early). Remember to check out the Domaine de la Courtade's winery.

Top growers to visit (see also p.134)

Château de Brégançon
639 route de Léoube, 83230 Bormes-les-Mimosas,
tel: 04 94 64 80 73
This magnificent *cru classé* estate, worked by the same family for seven generations, overlooks the sea and the islands of Porquerolles, Port Cros and Levant. Nearby is Fort Brégançon, the summer residence of French presidents, and the reason the coastline is unspoiled by development. The architecture is typically Provençal with tastings in beautiful vaulted cellars. Prices are reasonable. The white from Ugni Blanc and Rolle may not detain you but the rosés and reds are interesting *(B4)*.

Château de Selle
RD 73, 83460 Taradeau, tel: 04 94 47 57 57
This magnificent former residence of the Counts of Provence is one of the three celebrated Ott family domaines (as they say, "some like it Ott"). The wines and the welcome are exemplary. This is the place to buy the Coeur de Grain rosé from Cabernet, Grenache, and Cinsault. The château's white is appreciated by lovers of Sémillon while the red Comtes be Provence pleases fans of Cabernet. The Longue Garde speaks for itself, and the estate also produces a Vieux Marc de Rosé which is aged for six years in oak. The cave is in a former silkworm nursery containing wonderful old oak foudres. A star *cru classé* estate. *(D3: expensive)*

Finding a place to stay
You can stay at a number of châteaux in the area. Château du Rouët and Domaine des Planes (see left) both offer pleasant accommodation around Fréjus. Dining amidst the vines is also possible at Chez Bruno (see p.47) in Lorgues where truffles are the speciality. Hyères is a great place to stay too.

Côteaux Varois

The Varois vineyards cover some of the most attractive, rolling countryside in Provence. Vines give way to fields of lavender and forests of pines, olives, and oaks. The high Varois plateau is home to sleepy hillside villages and rocky escarpments; the vineyards are between the medieval town of Brignoles in the east and St-Maximin in the west, and stretch from Tavernes in the north to Méounes-les-Montrieux. This is one of the youngest appellations in the south of France and is one-tenth the size of the surrounding Côtes de Provence.

Coteaux Varois' green growers

Cooperatives dominate the Coteaux Varois – there are fourteen co-ops, representing about 400 growers – and most offer a good range of inexpensive, fresh, and fruity wines. The most interesting wines come from the seventy or so independent producers. Many are recently liberated from obligations to their village co-op; others are newcomers to the region who are investing heavily. Quality is improving at a dazzling rate and organic viticulture is virtually the norm, thanks to the Coteaux Varois' beneficial climate.

It has taken time for the appellation to shrug off its reputation for mediocrity. Part of the problem is historical. When the Coteaux Varois was excluded from the Côtes de Provence AC it was largely due to the Fédération de Coteaux Varois Caves Coopératives' reluctance to adopt appellation regulations. At the time it was more profitable for them to serve the *vin de table* market. AC status was finally granted in 1993. Another reason why the Coteaux Varois was not included in the Côtes de Provence appellation is geographical: the terroir is different.

What the wines are like

Although the Côtes de Provence surrounds the Coteaux Varois, the Varois vineyards are higher, about 300m (980 feet) in altitude, and clay-limestone soils dominate, with some sandy gravel and bauxite. The climate is continental, and harvesting occurs about two weeks later than in the Côtes de Provence.

Rosé is easily the most important style. Producers have finally shed the area's former *vin*

BELOW *One of many fountains in Barjols, a town nicknamed the Tivoli of Provence.*

ABOVE *Brignoles, where it once rained toads.*

de table reputation and the best wines represent good value for money. They aren't wines to keep, however: enjoy them young. Reds account for one quarter of output and whites just five per cent. Grape varieties are similar to those in Côtes de Provence but there are differences. Grenache and Cinsault dominate the rosés, whereas Tibouren, popular in the Côtes de Provence, doesn't feature here. To safeguard the Mediterranean identity of the reds, the use of Cabernet Sauvignon is more restricted here than in Côtes de Provence, and Grenache, Syrah, Mourvèdre or Cinsault must make up eighty per cent of the blend. The appellation also discourages barrel ageing, in particular the use of new wood. Rolle dominates the whites but unlike in Côtes de Provence, Grenache Blanc can be included.

Having fought off a reputation for *vins de table*, now Coteaux Varois has to decide how to respond to its latest sobriquet: "the new California". Will this help or hinder?

Travelling around

The Coteaux Varois vineyards are located north and south of the A8 between Brignoles in the east and St-Maximin-la-Ste-Baume in the west. The appellation is sandwiched between the Côtes de Provence and the vineyards of Mont Ste-Victoire. You can reach the Coteaux Varois wine country from Toulon or Marseille, in the south, via the A57/D43 to Brignoles or the A520/N560 to St-Maximin-la-Ste-Baume respectively. Alternatively, head east out of Aix-en-Provence on the A8 (La Provençale), direction Frèjus.

The best place to start discovering Varois wines is the eleventh-century Abbaye de La Celle in the heart of the hilltop wine village of La Celle outside Brignoles (*B3*). The appellation's attractive headquarters, the Maison des Vins des

Coteaux Varois, adjoins the abbey. There are 150 wines, an experimental vineyard with eighty-eight Provençal varieties (many of them rare), cloisters and a formal garden.

Then head south to the tiny village of Néoules (A3) where you will find the Domaine de Trians winery (see box p.54), and take in the Vallée du Gapeau and the Montrieux forest around Méounes. Continue up to La Roquebrussanne, stopping at Domaine du Loou (B3), and then around the 830m (2,700-foot) Montagne de la Loube, past Domaine de la Gayolle, to Tourves and on to St-Maximin (C4), where both Domaine du Deffends and Cellier de la Ste-Baume are located. Then head north to the villages of Brue-Auriac and Tavernes and east to Villacroze (D1). Villacroze is known for its caves and troglodyte château.

Nearby Tourtour, known as "the village in the sky", is perched in the pre-Alps overlooking the Var plain, and just north is the truffle capital, Aups. The route swings back through Salernes, home of the La Cavanne olive oil co-op, Sillans-la-Cascade, with its 40m (130-foot) waterfall, and on to the hillside town of Barjols (D3).

This former leather-tanning capital is dubbed the Tivoli of

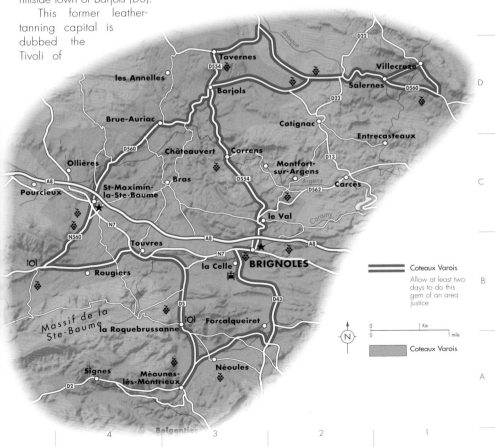

GROWERS IN COTEAUX VAROIS

Cellier de la Ste-Baume
RN7, 83470 St-Maximin
Tel: 04 94 78 03 97
This typical Provençal *cave coopérative* produces a good-value range, including the top red Cuvée Spéciale. *(C4: inexpensive)*

Château la Curnière
83670 Tavernes
Tel: 04 94 72 39 31
This elegant estate has its own chapel, *bastide* and *magnanerie* (silkworm nursery). *(D3: inexpensive)*

Château La Calisse
D560, 83670 Pontevès
Tel: 04 93 99 11 01
Buy from the Etoiles range. Ring ahead, afternoon visits preferred. *(D2: moderate)*

Château Thuerry
83690 Villecroze
Tel: 04 94 70 63 02
Buy the Cabernet-enriched Abeillons from this beautiful estate. *(D1: moderate)*

Domaine des Alysses
La Bas Deffend,
83670 Pontevès
Tel: 09 94 77 10 36
Organic with a reputation for original, thoughtfully-made wines. Buy full-bodied reds and crisp Chardonnay. *(D2: moderate)*

Domaine du Loou
D5, 83136 La Roquebrussanne
Tel: 04 94 86 94 97
Traditional, well-structured, old-vine reds are barrel-aged. *(B3: inexpensive)*

Domaine de Trians
Chemin des Rudelles, Néoules
Tel: 04 94 04 08 22
The red and white show what can be achieved in the appellation. *(A3: moderate)*

Provence on account of its fountains. The scenic D554 from Barjols to Le Val and Brignoles passes Château Miraval and goes through a long, picturesque ravine that takes in the hamlet of Châteauvert.

Since public transport is limited, this area is best discover by car and you should allow at least two days. Cycling is an option made more agreeable by the generally flat terrain around the plain to the south of the appellation. But, with vineyards between 250 and 500m (820 and 1,640 feet) in altitude, expect to climb up some steep hills, especially to the north.

Top growers in Coteaux Varois (*see also p.135*)

Château Miraval
83143 Le Val, tel: 04 94 86 46 8
Good-looking 300ha organic estate with American owners. (*C2: moderate*)

Château Triennes
RN560, 83860 Nans-les-Pins, tel: 04 94 78 91 46
This estate just makes *vins de pays*, the idea being to make wines from whatever expresses itself best in the vineyard. Varietal wines include an unmatched Viognier, a burgundy-style Chardonnay that betrays the owner's origins, and excellent Merlots, Cabernets, and Syrahs. Triennes also blends, with regard only to quality, not to rules. The best are Les Auréliens (Cabernet and Syrah) and St-Auguste (Cabernet, Syrah, and Merlot). The rosé is a pale and aromatic *vin gris* from Cinsault, Syrah and Merlot. If you buy from only one domaine, forget all that appellation jazz and take some Triennes home. (*B5: inexpensive to moderate*)

Domaine de la Gayolle
D205, 83170 La Celle, tel: 04 94 59 10 88
This domaine, between La Roquebrussanne and Tourves, has a remarkable eleventh-century stone chapel in the shape of a Greek cross, built on the remains of a fifth-century chapel from the era of the first Frankish sovereigns. The Brignoles museum has a

sarcophagus found here, the earliest Christian relic in France (c.175–225AD). Its varietal *vins de pays*, including Chardonnay and Cabernet Sauvignon, complement an AC range. Telephone ahead. (*B3: inexpensive to moderate*)

Finding a place to stay

If you want to brag that you've stayed in a town where it once rained toads, base yourself in Brignoles, where the hotels are inexpensive though not inspiring (*B2*; the curiously uncelebrated event took place in September 1973). Château de Nans, south of St-Maximin, provides attractive accommodation, with its pool, gardens, gastronomic restaurant and nicely refurbished rooms. It's overlooked by the Massif de la Ste-Baume and is across from the Ste-Baume golf course. Monsieur Brambeck will be happy to arrange a round or share tips on how best to explore the surrounding countryside. Alternatively, there's the cosy Provençal Auberge de la Loube in La Roquebrussanne (*B3*), with pretty rooms and regional cuisine.

Other things to do

Brignoles has an attractive medieval quarter and a quirky museum (Musée du Pays Brignoles, tel: 04 94 69 45 18) based in the twelfth-century Palais des Comtes de Provence. St-Maximin's main attraction is its splendid basilica and

BELOW *The outstanding secenery around Domaine Fontainbleu (see p.135).*

Cassis and Bandol

B andol and Cassis are picturesque ports between Toulon and
Marseille. Pleasure-seekers' yachts fill their harbours, and
cheerful, pastel-coloured restaurants and cafés line their seafronts.
Bandol is the undisputed capital of superior Provençal reds while
Cassis is famous for its distinctive white wine. Bandol's vineyards
cover an amphitheatre of slopes behind the town while the tallest cliff
in France, Cap Canaille, looms over those of Cassis. The route around
Cassis takes in amazing terraced vineyards where God is said to have
shed a tear and given birth to the local wine. If true, God has straw-
coloured tears with a herbal bouquet and salty tang.

LOCAL INFORMATION

TOURISM OFFICES: Allée Vivien
83150 Bandol
Tel: 04 94 29 41 35
Fax: 04 94 32 50 39
otbandol@bandol.fr
www.bandol.org

L'Oustau Calendal
Quai des Moulins
13260 Cassis
Tel: 04 42 01 71 17
Fax: 0004 42 01 28 31
omt@cassis.fr, www.cassis.fr

BIKE HIRE: Holiday Bikes
127 route de Marseille
83150 Bandol
Tel: 04 94 29 03 32
bandol@holiday-bikes.com
www.holiday-bikes.com

Le Tonneau de Bacchus
296 ave du 11 Novembre
83150 Bandol
Tel: 04 94 29 01 01
www.letonneaudebacchus.com

Académie de Bacchus
814 ave de Bruxelles
83500 La Seyne-sur-Mer
Tel: 04 94 87 33 17
www.academiedebacchus.com

The red and the white

Quite why Bandol developed a reputation for sturdy reds while Cassis busied itself with perfecting whites is something of a mystery. Perhaps the appetite for white wines in Cassis developed to complement a cuisine based around the local fishermen's catch, including sea anemones, a local speciality from the famed fiord-like rocky inlets, the *calanques*. Maybe the tradition for reds in Bandol happened because Bandol was historically the more important trading port and reds simply travelled better than whites. There are accounts in the eighteenth and nineteenth centuries of Bandol reds going as far as America and India, and improving with the sea voyage. And when Louis XV was asked the secret of his eternal youth, he replied "the wines of Bandol". The winemaking traditions of both towns were recognized early by the wine authorities. In fact, Cassis was the first AC in Provence (1936) while Bandol earned its AC just five years later.

What the wines are like

Bandol reds are generally *vins de garde*, spending eighteen months in oak and often requiring a decade before expressing themselves fully. Based on the thick-skinned, small-berried, and notoriously finicky Mourvèdre, they are drinkable, if somewhat aggressive, up to four years old and then pass through a dumb phase for a few years before becoming more mellow, complex, and interesting. Bandol rosés also emphasize Mourvèdre, although from younger vines. They're intended to accompany food, unlike the thirst-quenching rosés of the Côtes de Provence. The appellation also allows Grenache, Cinsault, and Syrah but the best reds are nearly pure Mourvèdre, with rich, firm, peppery, red- and black-berry flavours and a dark purple colour.

Cassis whites are straw-coloured, with floral and herbal aromas and a faintly salty tang. They are stronger and spicier than other Provençal whites and are based on Marsanne, Clairette, and Ugni Blanc, with some Sauvignon and Bourboulenc. At their best with food rather than as an apéritif, they should be drunk young. Some say they are an acquired taste and are overpriced, but they certainly have character.

Syrah is excluded from the permitted grape varieties for Cassis reds, which can be aged, but not for as long as Bandol.

Squeezed between Bandol and Cassis are the Le Bassin du Beausset vineyards of the Côtes de Provence appellation. These wines have much in common with their kin along La Bordure Maritime with more limestone soils, instead of granite and schist.

Travelling around

Bandol and Cassis are easily reached from big neighbours Marseille and Toulon, to the east and west respectively. Or, if you're coming from Aix-en-Provence, follow the A52/A50 south. Renting a bike is an option in both Bandol and Cassis. You can even walk the wine route around Cassis. Plan on spending at least two days discovering the wines of both towns.

The Bandol route has spectacular views of the Mediterranean from vineyards just inland on a natural amphitheatre of slopes rising 400m (1,300 feet) behind Bandol. East of Bandol, the route takes in pretty Ollioules – famous for France's largest flower market – and the dramatic limestone Gorges d'Ollioules. The village of Le Beausset, with its pretty triangular "square", and the fortified hilltop village of Le Castellet, its narrow streets lined with touristy cafés,

WHERE TO STAY AND EAT

Le Chanteplage
place de l'Appel du 18 Juin
83270 Les Lecques
Tel: 04 94 26 16 55
Fax: 04 94 26 25 71

Hôtel Key Largo
19 Corniche Bonaparte
83150 Bandol
Tel: 04 94 29 46 93
Fax: 04 94 32 49 03

Les Oliviers
Hôtel Ile Rousse
17 blvd Louis Lumière
83150 Bandol
Tel: 04 94 29 33 00

Les Roches Blanches
route des Calanques
13260 Cassis
Tel: 04 42 01 09 30
Fax: 04 42 01 94 23
hotel@roches-blanches-cassis.com
www.roches-blanches-cassis.com

Bandol
Allow two days to make the most of this rich vinous area

Cassis
One day for this group of growers

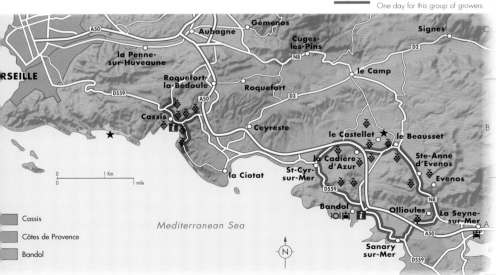

Cassis

Côtes de Provence

Bandol

Mediterranean Sea

GROWERS IN BANDOL

Château Ste-Anne
83330 Ste-Anne d'Evenos
Tel: 04 94 90 35 40
Set in wooded parkland, this faces the astonishing Evenos cliffs. All organic, of the two red *cuvées*, the superior Collection contains the most Mourvèdre. *(B1: expensive)*

Domaine de L'Hermitage
Le Rouve BP 41, 83330
Le Beausset, Tel: 04 94 98 71 31
Louis XV was a big fan of this organic domaine. The reds are the stars of this exemplary winery. *(B1: expensive)*

Domaine de Souviou
RN8, 83330 Le Beausset
Tel: 04 94 90 57 63
The idyllic setting for the summer Les Vespérales concerts, the reds steal the show but don't miss the barrel-aged white. *(B1: moderate)*

Domaine Tempier
83330 Le Plan-de-Castellet
Tel: 04 94 98 70 21
Arguably the historic centre of the appellation and its driving force. Tempier produces three single-vineyard reds, with increasing amounts of Mourvèdre. *(B2: expensive)*

Domaine Terrebrune
chemin de la Tourelle, 83190
Ollioules, Tel: 04 94 74 01 30
On one of the appellation's best sites, this estate produces exemplary reds. You can dine at the domaine's restaurant, La Table du Vigneron. *(A1: expensive)*

Domaine de la Tour du Bon
83330 Le Brûlat-du-Castellet
Tel: 04 94 32 61 62
This rising star makes an accessible red that's lighter on Mourvèdre than usual. The classy, top red is nearly pure Mourvèdre. *(B2: moderate)*

restaurants, galleries, and shops, are also on the route. A walk up to Le Castellet's tenth-century castle, which dominates the horizon, rewards with its panoramic views; check out the Romanesque chapel of Notre-Dame-du-Beausset-Vieux, too. The route crosses the plateau du Camp to St-Cyr-sur-Mer and ends near the beaches of the Golfe des Lecques west of Bandol.

The Cassis route takes in some of the most stunning vineyards in Provence: those overlooking Cassis on the terraced slopes of Cap Canaille. Beginning just off the A50 (junction 8), 2.5km (1.5 miles) along the D559 at the beautifully restored eighteenth-century Château de Fontcreuse, the route takes in the hills around the bay of Cassis.

Top grower in Bandol and Cassis (*see also* p.135)
Domaine de La Laidière
426 chemin de Font-Vive, 83330 Ste-Anne d'Evenos,
tel: 04 94 90 37 07
The Estienne family have owned this top estate above Ste-Anne d'Evenos for about ten generations. They make Bandol in all three colours and helped launch the appellation. Buy the very fine, traditional Cuvée Spéciale, with ninety per cent Mourvèdre. The red Tradition is also admirable (and cheaper). This domaine has a reputation for its whites, so try the floral and fruity Ugni Blanc-Clairette. Its rosé is made to go with food and is big on flavour. *(B1: moderate to expensive)*

Finding a place to stay
Base yourself in either town or somewhere in between, like Les Lecques or its lively old town, St-Cyr-sur-Mer *(B2)*. There's the

two-star Le Chanteplage on the seafront in Les Lecques with great views. In Bandol, you can economise by staying at the pleasant sixteen-room Hôtel Key Largo with views over the Ile de Bendor. Spend what you save at the excellent Les Oliviers restaurant at the Hôtel Ile Rousse. Jean-Paul Lanyou is the talented *chef de cuisine* and Christophe Carreau is the knowledgeable and genial sommelier.

A good place to start discovering Bandol's wines is in the company of Frédéric Robin at the splendid Le Tonneau de Bacchus wine emporium. The most spectacular (and expensive) hotel in Cassis is the four-star Les Roches Blanches, perched over the bay. You'll find lots of enticing restaurants in Cassis along the Quai des Baux and some more affordable options in the back streets away from the harbour.

Other things to do

A favourite activity in Cassis is a boat trip to the *calanques*. Make sure your boat lets you off, and don't miss the chance to swim in the clear emerald waters below the cliffs. The farthest *calanque* from Cassis, and the most beautiful, is En-Vau. The tourist office in Cassis can provide details of organized trips and boat rentals.

Travelling in the opposite direction, the stunning 17km (10-mile) Corniche des Crêtes to La Ciotat takes in hairpin bends and vertiginous views (*B3*). Just east of Bandol at La Seyne-sur-Mer you can brush up your wine tasting skills with a tasting course at the Académie de Bacchus (*A1*).

GROWERS IN CASSIS

Clos Ste-Magdeleine
ave du Revestel, 13260
Cassis, Tel: 04 42 01 70 28
Ring ahead to avoid missing this astonishingly attractive Art Deco property's superior whites and rosés.
(*B3: moderate to expensive*)

Domaine du Bagnol
12 ave de Provence, 13260
Cassis, Tel: 04 42 01 78 05
At the foot of Cap Canaille. Try the flavourful white Cassis in its youth, and the rare red Cassis. (*B3: inexpensive to moderate*)

Domaine du Paternel
11 Route de la Ciotat, 13260
Cassis, Tel: 04 42 01 77 03
A traditionalist whose rich white Cassis is among the region's best with great ageing potential.
(*B3: moderate*)

LEFT *The vineyards of Clos Ste-Magdeleine in Cassis.*

BELOW *The bay of Bandol – explore the town as well.*

Ste-Victoire and Palette

Cézanne's beloved Mont Ste-Victoire dominates the skyline of the new Ste-Victoire appellation. Many of the domaines are at the foot of its dramatic 10km (6-mile) long white cliff. Ste-Victoire's neighbour is tiny, curious, and prestigious Palette. This is the smallest AC in Provence with just three independent producers and a co-op. It's also one of the oldest. Palette's distinctive and sought-after wines are made from a hotchpotch of traditional Provençal varieties. Rosés dominate Ste-Victoire output whereas white is the main colour in Palette. The most rare of all are the long-lived Palette reds.

Wines from the hills

The Ste-Victoire terroir extends from the foothills of Mont Ste-Victoire in the north across the Arc Valley and spills over Mount Aurélien to the south; it's bordered to the east by the Coteaux Varois and to the west by Palette and the Coteaux d'Aix-en-Provence. The twenty-three independent producers and five cooperatives have a strong sense of identity and mission; however, there's not that much to distinguish them from their large neighbours, except lower yields. It really depends on the individual *vigneron*.

BELOW *The Coteaux d'Aix estate of Domaine de Beaulieu, in Rogues.*

Obscure, expensive, and *recherché* describes Palette. In fact, it's easy to overlook the entire appellation, which is on a hillside just east of the beautiful city of Aix. Curiously, there's really only ever been one significant producer, the reputable Château Simone, and it's been in the same family for seven generations (*see* p.63). The Carmelite sisterhood of Aix planted Château Simone's vineyards in the sixteenth century and hewed the cellars out of the hillside. Today, at least half of Palette's output goes straight to Aix's top restaurants while the remainder is sold on the spot or exported.

Palette was granted AC status in 1948, making it a member of the exclusive *Association 50 ans d'AOC Provençales* (the Provençal AOCs' over-fifties club), which includes Bellet, Bandol, and Cassis. A combination of particular terroir and superior wine accounts for its early recognition.

Travelling around

Plan to spend two or three days exploring Ste-Victoire and Palette, beginning your tour of Ste-Victoire in the ancient town of Trets (*B2*). Here the château houses the appellation's smart showroom, La Maison des Vins de la Ste-Victoire, and to the east of the town you will find the wineries of Chateau Ferry Lacombe and Mas de Cadenet. Check out Trets' Romanesque church and medieval ramparts, too. Then head to the wine village of Pourcieux, shaded by plane trees, where *vigneronss'* houses surround the Château du Pourcieux winery. Follow the route to Pourrières, with its views over Ste-Victoire, taking in Domaine Silvy, before travelling on to the perched village of Puyloubier with its Foreign Legion retirement farm and arts complex (tel: 04 42 66 38 20). There's a panoramic view over the vineyards, the plain and Mont Ste-Victoire. Here you can visit the domaines of Richaume and St-Ser and the châteaux of Coussin and Baron George. The route continues to the pretty Palette villages of Le Tholonet and Meyreuil, where you will find the wineries of châteaux Cremade and Meyreuil, before heading along the busy N7 back towards Trets.

The Palette wine route is one of the smallest in Provence and one of the most spectacular. The route follows Cézanne's footsteps through landscapes he immortalized – he painted Mont Ste-Victoire at least sixty times from the village of Le Tholonet alone. Château Simone and others are around the village of Meyreuil. This route can be done by car, bike or on foot, but if cycling, try to stay off the N7.

What the wines are like

Until recently, Ste-Victoire was part of the mammoth Côtes de Provence appellation. The wines have much in common and you'd be hard pushed to distinguish one from the other. As in Côtes de Provence, rosés dominate production. Seventy per cent of Ste-Victoire is rosé, the rest is red with a little white. Ste-Victoire represents fifteen per cent, or 13.3 million bottles, of the total annual Côtes de Provence output. This dwarfs the figure

Ste-Victoire and Palette
Two or three days should do
justice to the wineries of both
Ste-Victoire and Palette

Palette

0   5 Km
0   5 miles

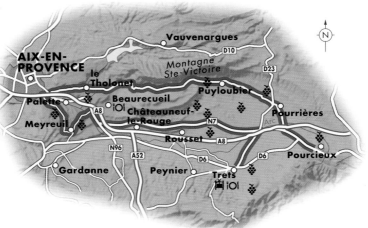

for Palette of 180,000 bottles. Palette's vineyards are just east of Aix-en-Provence on an amphitheatre of well-exposed limestone terraces facing north towards Mont Ste-Victoire. They're surrounded by pine forests and include the usual Provençal vines, plus a few more obscure and unidentifiable varieties. Maritime influences are present but the vineyards are protected from the worst of the Mistral. This combination of geology and climate partly explains why Palette was recognized early for AC status. That its wines are unique may be the other reason.

Palette whites are based on Clairette with additions of Grenache Blanc and Ugni Blanc. Some pretty unconventional varieties like Picpoul and Furmint, the latter hailing originally from Hungary, may be in the blend. They may be matured in oak too, and can be aged for a couple of years. Some Palette rosés are oak-aged, too, but they tend to be more like light reds in structure and flavour: full, fruity, and richly aromatic.

The reds are the most remarkable Palette wines. They're based on Grenache, Mourvèdre, and Cinsault with up to fifteen other varieties like the rare Castet, Manosquin, Branforquas, and Picpoul Noir. Some varieties have no names and the effect in the glass is complex. The reds are aged in barrels, not for the oak, but for the gentle oxidation that old oak can give, and they don't leave the domaine until two or three years after the vintage. They are meaty, firm and spicy. As they're expensive, just buy the best vintages. The most recent are 2001, 1998, and 1997. The 1995 and 1993, two other great years, should be just about ready to drink.

Top growers in Ste-Victoire and Palette (*see also* p.136)
Château Grand'Boise
route de la Grisole, 13530 Trets, tel: 04 42 29 22 95
This picturesque seventeenth-century hillside property on the slopes of Mount Aurélien is set in nearly 400ha of pine and oak

forest facing Mont Ste-Victoire. Jan Aarsoe Nielsen has owned the place since 1990. Try Cuvée Mazarine, produced in all three colours in the best years. The white is nearly pure Sémillon. Modern, well-made wines. (*A2: inexpensive to moderate*)

Domaine Richaume
13114 Puyloubier, tel: 04 42 66 31 27
This organic domaine is flanked by Mont Ste-Victoire and produces arguably the finest wines in the area. Reds are emphasized (eighty per cent of production) with Cabernet and Syrah used for the best blend, Cuvée Columelle. The Clairette and Rolle-based whites are also excellent, with honey, mineral, and floral notes. The non-appellation Viognier and Sauvignon are very good too. Olive oil is also produced. Telephone ahead. (*B2: expensive*)

Château Simone
Chemin Simone, 13590 Meyreuil, tel: 04 42 66 92 58, www.chateau-simone.fr, mail@chateau-simone.com
The most famous name in Palette. This beautiful property with astonishing sixteenth-century vaulted cellars has 23ha of organic vineyards, including some 100-year-old vines. It produces full-bodied red *vins de garde*, two interesting whites, and an old-fashioned rosé which is heavier, more complex, more deeply-coloured and more alcoholic than any other in Provence. Their wines are original and always in great demand, so they are expensive. (*B4*)

Finding a place to stay
Staying in Aix makes sense for discovering these two appellations (*see* p.68). Or there are two three-star options in Beaureceuil just east of Aix (*B3*). At Mas de la Bertrande most of the ten rooms have views of Mont Ste-Victoire; there's a pool and restaurant as well. The Relais Ste-Victoire is the same size, with a pool, jacuzzi and fine dining with a Michelin star. If you're on the wine route, try Le Clos Gourmand in Trets.

Coteaux d'Aix-en-Provence

The Coteaux d'Aix-en-Provence has had a love affair with Cabernet Sauvignon since the mid-1960s and produces seriously good examples. They're some of the best value wines in Provence. The vineyards cover landscapes painted by Aix's most famous son, Paul Cézanne; the citizens mocked him during his life but it's hard to hold that against the charming erstwhile capital of Provence.

The land of the Mistral

The Coteaux d'Aix-en-Provence is easily the second-largest appellation in Provence, and one of the youngest – it gained AC standing in 1985. Its existence is attributed to the efforts of one Georges Brunet, formerly of Château Vignelaure at Rians (see p.68). He was the first to bring Cabernet into the region from Bordeaux and blended it with Syrah. His sought-after wines earned a reputation beyond Provence and convinced the authorities (and other vignerons) of the merits of this terroir. There was disappointment when the region failed to get AC status in 1977, especially as Côtes de Provence was promoted that year. Undeterred, vignerons embraced quality, replanted vineyards, and today produce genuine terroir wines, albeit with enormous variations in style. There are around seventy independent producers across this broad and dispersed appellation.

The river Durance marks the northern limit of the terroir. Beyond is the forest of the Petit Luberon, the lower chain of the Montagne du Luberon. The countryside around the Durance is particularly beautiful and it's easy to forget that the river used to be counted as one of the three "plagues" of Provence, the other two being the Mistral and the parliament at Aix. The terroir is dominated by clay and limestone, outcropping in places, with sandier soil towards the Mediterranean. The Mistral blows forcefully through the succession of mountain chains that traverses the landscape from east to west. In between are plateaus, plains, and fertile valleys. Variations in temperature mean that harvesting begins up to a month earlier in the south than in the north.

What the wines are like

The red wines come in two styles: those intended for early drinking and the serious vins de garde. In the first category are immediately approachable and appealingly fruity reds, not unlike those of the southern Côtes de Rhône or the Côtes de Provence. In the second category are the wines making the appellation's reputation today: the Bordeaux-style reds. These wines are for ageing and are worth seeking out. They're

LOCAL INFORMATION

Office de Tourisme
place du Général De Gaulle
13100 Aix-en-Provence
Tel: 04 42 16 11 61
Fax: 04 42 16 11 62
info@aixenprovencetourism.com
www.aixenprovencetourism.com

Office de Tourisme
56 cours Gimon
13300 Salon-en-Provence
Tel: 04 90 56 27 60
Fax: 04 90 56 77 09
otsalon@visitprovence.com

typically a blend of Cabernet, Syrah, and Grenache. The best probably contain more Cabernet than the rules allow.

Given the appetite for enjoyable summer drinking, it's not surprising that rosé production slightly exceeds that of reds. The rosés are fruitier and not quite so bone dry as other Provençal pinks. Only a tiny amount of white wine is produced. The most elegant dry whites come from the northerly vineyards around the Durance. These are Clairette, Rolle, Bourboulenc, and Sémillon blends. Grenache Blanc makes it into the blend further south. The white wines of the neighbouring Les Baux appellation are also designated Coteaux d'Aix-en-Provence (see p.69).

Finding a place to stay

The eighteenth-century Grand Hôtel Nègre-Coste on the Cours Mirabeau is a comfortable, centrally located, three-star hotel close to Aix's café institution, Les Deux Garçons. There are restaurants, cafés, bookshops, and antique fountains on the street below. Alternatively there's the four-star Villa Gallici just north of the centre, a luxury Relais & Châteaux member. Dining out should include a meal at Aix's Le Clos de la Violette. This Michelin-two-star restaurant in the north of town is for lovers of seriously flavourful Provençal cuisine and mouth-watering desserts. Or, follow your nose around the place de Cardeurs next to the Hôtel de Ville or head down rue de la Verrerie to place Ramus where there are all kinds of tempting restaurants.

TRIP TO A THEME PARK

Village des Automates
RN7, 13760 St Cannat
Tel: 04 42 57 30 30
If the children are in tow, the Village des Automates is a theme park with over 500 robotic characters. It's between St-Cannat and Aix.

BELOW *Mont Ste-Victoire, a landmark as much photographed as painted.*

Travelling around

If you're based in Aix, you can start exploring wine country right away. Château de la Gaude is just 5km (3 miles) from the centre. To begin the wine route proper, head to historic Rians east of Aix (*C8*), where pretty streets spiral around the town's ancient fortress tower. Château Vignelaure just outside Rians is a must. This estate is beside the Canal de Provence and it's where the appellation began. Head west along the Durance Valley and you're in the most northerly vineyards in the appellation. You pass through the fortified villages of Peyrolles and Jouques, home to Château Revelette. Nearby Meyrargues shouldn't be missed. It has an impressive tenth-century hilltop château and also the remains of a Roman

═══ Coteaux d'Aix-en-Provence
Plan to spend at least three
days exploring Aix and the
surrounding wine country

aqueduct. Still heading northwest, turn off for the perched village of Rognes, where Château Beaulieu, the largest estate in the appellation is based (see p.136). Getting back onto the main road, continue to La Roque d'Anthéron, with its pretty canals, and visit the nearby Abbaye de Silvacane. Follow the D561 out of La Roque d'Anthéron and join the N7 to take in the domaines between Cazan and Aix, pausing first to visit Château Bas in Vernégues. Along the way, you can see Château Virant and Commanderie de la Bargemone in St-Cannat – the perfect opportunity to leave the busy N7.

Over in the west, the gentrified Salon-de-Provence (D1), that other smart Provençal bourg, marks the western limit of the Coteaux d'Aix. Between Salon and the vast Etang de Berre lagoon to the south are three attractive wine villages: Grans, Lançon-Provence and Cornillon-Confoux. There's not much to detain you to the industrial south of the étang, except pretty Martigues with its quays and canals (dubbed "little Venice") and the coastline west of Carry-le-Rouet where the Chaîne de l'Estaque plunges into the Mediterranean.

GROWERS IN COTEAUX D'AIX-EN-PROVENCE

Château Revelette
13490 Jouques
Tel: 04 42 63 75 43 *(C7: moderate)*

Château de Fonscolombe
13610 Le Puy-Ste-Réparade,
Tel: 04 42 61 70 00 *(D5: inexpensive to moderate)*

Château La Coste
13610 Le Puy-Ste-Réparade
Tel: 04 42 61 89 98 *(D5: inexpensive to moderate)*

Château de Calissanne
13680 Lançon-de-Provence
Tel: 04 90 42 63 03 *(C2: moderate to expensive)*

Château Virant
13680 Lançon-de-Provence
Tel: 04 90 42 44 47 *(C2: inexpensive)*

Commanderie de la Bargemone
13760 St-Cannat
Tel: 04 42 57 22 44 *(D4: moderate)*

Château de Beaupré
13760 St-Cannat
Tel: 04 42 57 33 59 *(D4: moderate)*

Château du Seuil
13540 Puyricard
Tel: 04 42 92 15 99 *(C5: moderate to expensive)*

Château de la Gaude
13100 Aix-en-Provence
Tel: 04 42 21 64 19 *(B5: inexpensive to moderate)*

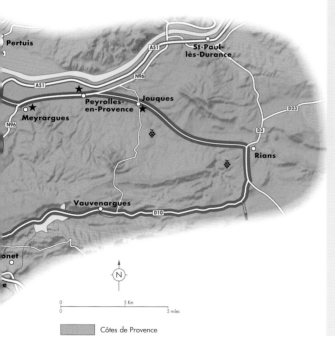

Côtes de Provence

WHERE TO STAY

Grand Hôtel Nègre-Coste
33 Cours Mirabeau
13100 Aix-en-Provence
Tel: 04 42 27 74 22
Fax: 04 42 26 80 93

Villa Gallici
ave de la Violette
13100 Aix-en-Provence
Tel: 04 42 23 29 23
Fax: 04 42 96 30 45
gallici@relaischateaux.fr

Le Clos de la Violette
10 ave de la Violette
13100 Aix-en-Provence
Tel: 04 42 23 30 71
Fax: 04 42 21 93 03

ALSO LOOK OUT FOR:
Maison de Nostradamus
11 rue de Nostradamus
13300 Salon-de-
Provence
Tel: 04 90 56 64 31

Other things to do
If you want to explore historic Aix, the leafy Cours Mirabeau is the best place to begin. Fans of ghost towns should check out Vieux Vernègues (*B3*). This medieval village was wholly destroyed in an earthquake in 1909. If you're into the occult, visit the house of Nostradamus in Salon-de-Provence.

Miramas is an attractive town on the northern edge of the vast Etang de Berre lagoon. Close by is the fortified village of Miramas-le-Vieux, and St-Chamas with its impressive Baroque church. Pont Flavian, which crosses a stream just south of St-Chamas, is one of the best-preserved Roman bridges anywhere. As you follow the route to St-Cannat, you have a chance to visit Château Le Barben, a beautiful fortress château with exquisite tapestries, period furniture, and a zoo. Nearby Lambesc is the former seat of the Provençal parliament and is noted for its seventeenth- and eighteenth-century town houses.

Top producers in Coteaux d'Aix-en-Provence
(*see* also p.136)
Château Beaulieu
13840 Rognes, tel: 04 42 50 20 19, contact@chateau beaulieu.fr
Set in formal gardens, this estate is the largest in the appellation. The restored château, some of which dates back to the twelfth century, has been in the same family for four generations. The 250ha vineyard covers volcanic soils across a crater in the Trévaresse chain, epicentre of the 1909 earthquake that devastated nearby Rognes and La Roque-d'Anthéron. The wines, in order of excellence, are La Provençale, Château Beaulieu, and Cuvée Bérengère. The Domaine Robert wines are organic while the Seigneurie label denotes *vins de pays*. (*D4: inexpensive to moderate*)

Château Vignelaure
route de Jouques, 83560 Rians, tel: 04 94 37 21 10
This estate has had its ups and downs since Georges Brunet introduced Cabernet here in the 1960s. His wines quickly earned an international reputation, but changes in ownership since saw standards decline. The O'Briens acquired the estate in the 1990s and have revived its fortunes. At 400m (1,300 feet) in altitude, the organic vineyards cover some of the highest terrain in the appellation.

The top Cabernet-dominated château reds, worthy of a decade of ageing, show that the estate has recovered its former glory. The domaine wines are excellent too. The cellars have an impressive collection of contemporary art with works by Buffet, Arman, Miro, César, and Cartier-Bresson. (*C8: moderate*)

Les Baux-de-Provence

Les Baux is Provence at its most beautiful and beguiling. The craggy, limestone Les Alpilles massif dominates the landscape. Scrubby garrigue and olive trees cover its slopes. At its centre looms the ruined citadel of Les Baux, overlooking the mysterious Val d'Enfer – Hell Valley – with its weird rocks, troglodyte caves and abandoned quarries. Vincent Van Gogh sought refuge from the world here, Daudet wrote his sentimental *Lettres de Mon Moulin* (*Letters from my Windmill*) nearby and Nostradamus was born here.

Wine from a distinctive terroir

Winemakers of Les Baux-de-Provence have long insisted on the distinctiveness of their terroir, even if the wine authorities took years to realize what all the fuss was about. Until 1995 the area was just another part of the sprawling Coteaux d'Aix-en-Provence. Yet, there's no mistaking what makes Les Baux different: concentration and finesse.

The vineyards are neatly defined on the northern and southern slopes of the Alpilles hills. The soil is limestone, with sandy marl and bauxite outcrops to the north and clay on the southern slopes. Cabernet and Syrah prefer the cooler north and the Mediterranean varieties thrive in the warmer south, where harvests can be as much as two weeks earlier. The southern wines are a bit more rustic and a little less refined than those in the north, but none the worse for being different.

Green dream

Les Baux-de-Provence is one of the most environmentally friendly appellations anywhere. You'd be hard pushed to find any artificial fertilizer or herbicide kicking around the domaines featured here. Thanks to the dry, warm climate and the Mistral – which is blustery in these parts – most producers can eschew non-organic treatments.

What the wines are like

The irony of Les Baux is that, having spent a decade arguing about its distinctiveness, the top producer is firmly excluded from the appellation. Not that he could care less. The cult winemaker Eloi Dürrbach at Domaine de Trévallon does as he pleases, usually with

LEFT *This old château houses a vinotheque.*

BELOW *Alternative souvenirs at Château d'Estoublon in Fontvieille.*

LEFT *The Abbaye de Montmajour, a medieval abbey near Daudet's windmill.*

LOCAL INFORMATION

Office de Tourisme
place Jean Jaurès
13210 St-Rémy-de-
Provence
Tel: 04 90 92 05 22
Fax: 04 90 92 38 52
www.saintremy-
de-provence.com

Office de Tourisme
Impasse du Château
13520 Les Baux-de-
Provence
Tel: 04 90 54 34 39
Fax: 04 90 54 51 15
tourisme@
lesbauxdeprovence.com
www.lesbauxdeprovence.com

BIKE HIRE: Karimoto
29 ave de Fauconnet
13210 St-Rémy-de-
Provence
Tel: 04 90 92 54 00
Fax: 04 40 92 54 54

too much Cabernet and not enough Grenache for INAO's liking. He makes arguably the finest (and most expensive) *vins de pays* in France. But the reputation of the non-conformist Dürrbach shouldn't eclipse the supremely well made and more affordable wines produced by the likes of Colette and Jean-Pierre Peyraud at Château Romanin and others (*see* p.72).

There are two styles of red, those for early drinking and the more serious *vins de garde*. The former have much in common with the lighter, fruity reds of Provence or the southern Côtes du Rhône. The latter are rich and meaty, with spicy red and black fruit aromas. They compare well with the more pricey reds of Bandol, especially those with lots of Mourvèdre in the blend.

The rosés use the same varieties as the reds, though the blends vary enormously. At least fifty per cent of the blend must be *saignée* (literally "bled" from the red wine vats before the colour has had much time to develop) and the results are fruity and flavourful.

There's no white wine appellation for Les Baux at present, though whites with the appropriate varieties can be labelled Coteaux d'Aix-en-Provence. This may change in the next few years. Avant-garde producers have been spotted planting Marsanne and Roussanne, from the northern Rhône, in anticipation of a white Les Baux AC. You'll find prototypes labelled *vin de pays* and you should buy them before AC status ups the price.

Travelling around

You can visit most of the dozen notable producers in this region in a couple of days. Your wine route could begin in Mouriès, the French olive capital in the southeast of the appellation, where you'll find the Mas de Gourgonnier winery. Then head north on the D24 to Eygalières, with its ruined château and panoramic views, dropping by Domaine de la Vallongue along the way. Go west to picturesque St-Rémy-de-Provence, home of the progressive Château Romanin, and domaines Hauvette and Terres Blanche.

A detour into the Alpilles takes in Les Antiques, Ganlum, and Les Baux itself. The route out of Les Baux to Maillane, home of Provence's favourite poet, Frédéric Mistral, passes through the Val d'Enfer. Heading west, visit Château d'Estoublon at Fontvieille, and make time for the producers around St-Etienne-du-Grès (B4), including the lengendary Domaine de Trévallon and Château Dalmeran.

The must-see Roman relics at Les Antiques and the important Celtic settlement of Glanum are on the most sensational route in Provence: the D5 from St Rémy to Les Baux. Near Daudet's windmill on the Arles road is Montmajour, an outstanding medieval monastery. Olive trees vastly outnumber vines (this is

French olive heartland) and there are just a dozen *vignerons* around Les Baux, including the inspiring Mas de la Dame and Mas Ste-Berthe. They make some of the best reds in Provence.

Alternative modes of transport

Cycling around Les Baux is one option; it's a great way to see the countryside and it excuses you from buying too many expensive bottles along the way. You can rent a bike in St-Rémy. If you prefer a more leisurely pace, you can hike the GR6 trail, which traverses the Alpilles and passes through Les Baux. However, you'll want to take the car if you also plan to visit Avignon, Arles or nearby Salon.

Top growers in Les Baux-de-Provence
Château Romanin
13210 St-Rémy-de-Provence, tel: 04 90 92 45 87, contact@romanin.com, www.romanin.com

This large, welcoming Biodynamic estate has a remarkable 2,000 square-metre (6,560 square-feet) cathedral-like cave hewn from the rock, with sun and moon symbols in the vinification and maturing parts of the cellar respectively. There's a lovely reception area, too. Two *cuvées* in each colour are made: youthful La Chapelle de Romanin, and Château Romanin from older vines. Reds are based on Cabernet and Syrah (La

Les Baux-de-Provence
A couple of days will allow you to visit the key producers in this fascinating area

Les Baux-de-Provence

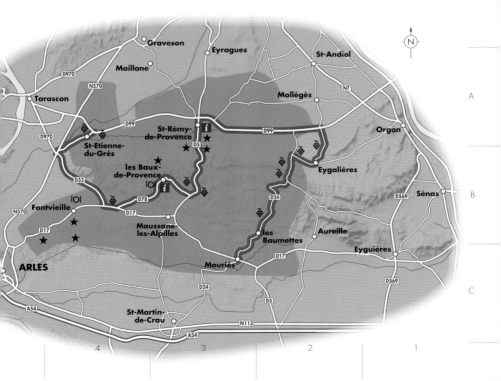

WHERE TO STAY AND EAT

Le Prince Noir
rue de L'Orme
13520 Les Baux-
de-Provence
Tel: 04 90 54 34 41

L'Oustau de Baumanière
route d'Arles, CD27
13520 Les Baux-
de-Provence
Tel: 04 90 54 33 07

La Regalido
118 rue Mistral
13990 Fontvieille
Tel: 04 90 54 60 22

ABOVE *Olive trees near Les Baux, producing another southern staple.*

RIGHT *One of Barjols' many fountains (see p.53).*

Chapelle includes seven varieties). The young whites blend Bourboulenc and Ugni Blanc while the château whites are made from Rolle and Sauvignon. The "Jean le Troubadour" *vins de pays* are excellent value. Le Coeur de Romanin is the top, expensive Les Baux red. There's an informative 2km (1.2-mile) educational trail around the vineyards, too.
(*A3: inexpensive to expensive*)

Domaine de Trévallon
ave ND du Château, 13103 St-Etienne-du-Grès,
tel: 04 90 49 06 00, trevallon@wanadoo.fr,
www.trevallon.com
This non-conformist, organic estate produces probably the best *vins de pays* in France. An over-abundance of Cabernet and Syrah and an absence of Grenache means Eloi Dürrbach's wines are excluded from the appellation. The reds are well-structured, rich, and sophisticated *vins de garde*. Some flavourful Marsanne and Roussanne whites are also made. The exacting owner was so unsatisfied with the 2002 vintage that, except for some Chardonnay harvested before the rains, he made no wine that year. Make an appointment. (*A4: expensive to very expensive*)

Mas de la Dame
13520 Les Baux-de-Provence, tel: 04 90 54 32 24
masdeladame@masdeladame.com, www.masdeladame.com
One of the oldest and best estates in Les Baux. It's organic, too. Van Gogh's 1889 "Mas Provençal" depicts the place. The reds come in three cuvées: Réserve, Coin Caché, and La Stèle, from

the oldest vines. There's also Blanc des Roches (Sémillon, Clairette, and Rolle), Sémillon-dominated Coin Caché, and Rolle La Stèle. Olives are also cultivated and nearby Maussane has a highly rated olive oil cooperative. (*B3: moderate*)

Finding a place to stay
You can base yourself in Les Baux, which is best out of season. There's the funky Le Prince Noir – bed and breakfast in an artist's house that's the highest residence in Les Baux. Or just outside the village there's the ultimate treat: the very expensive L'Oustau de Baumanière, a restored Provençal farmhouse with a two-Michelin-star restaurant.

The president of the Les Baux *syndicat* runs it and the wine list boasts some 100,000 bottles, so you should find something to go with your *raviolis de truffes aux poireaux* or *filets de rougets au basilic*. Alternatively, La Regalido is a luxury Relais & Châteaux hotel in a renovated windmill at Fontvieille with an *haut cuisine* restaurant.

Other things to do
The biggest local attraction is the Cathédrale d'Images. This sound and light show is staged in an abandoned quarry in the Val d'Enfer. Don't miss the nearby Pavillon de la Reine Jeanne, a pretty renaissance garden folly.

Daudet's windmill contains a museum about the writer, but more interesting are the Roman Vestiges de Caparon, 2km (1.2 miles) away. Van Gogh's asylum is actually the beautiful monastery of St-Paul-de-Mausole between St-Rémy and Les Baux. Nearby is the eighth-century Mas de la Pyramide, a troglodyte Provençal farmhouse.

St-Rémy is a pretty place north of Les Baux with an unspoiled old town, many museums and a long association with artists. Van Gogh spent his last days here and painted some of his best known works, such as "Yellow Cornfield" (1889) and "Still Life with Iris" (1890) while in the area. The Centre d'Art Présence Van Gogh in the beautiful eighteenth-century Hôtel d'Estrine, a former Grimaldi home, contains a permanent exhibition of photos and documents, plus a video on the artist's life (the museum is open from March to December, Tuesday to Sunday, tel: 04 90 92 34 72).

St-Rémy's collection of Celtic, Greek, and Roman artefacts from the Glanum archaeological site are on display at the interesting Musée Archéologique, located in another grand St-Rémy building, the fifteenth-century Hôtel de Sade (open from April to December, tel: 04 90 92 64 04).

GROWERS IN LES BAUX-DE-PROVENCE

Domaine Hauvette
chemin du Trou-des-Boeufs
13210 St-Rémy-de-Provence
Tel: 04 90 92 03 90 *(A3: moderate to expensive)*

Mas Ste-Berthe
13520 Les Baux-de-Provence
Tel: 04 90 54 39 01 *(B3: inexpensive)*

Mas du Gourgonnier
13890 Mouriès
Tel: 04 90 47 50 45 *(B3)*

Château d'Estoublon
route de Maussane
13990 Fontvieille
Tel: 04 90 54 64 00 *(B4)*

Château Dalmeran
13103 St-Etienne-du-Grès
Tel: 04 90 49 04 04 *(A4)*

Domaine Terres Blanches
13210 St-Rémy-de-Provence
Tel: 04 90 95 91 66 *(A3)*

Domaine de la Vallongue
13810 Eygalières
Tel: 04 90 95 91 70 *(B2)*

PRICES: moderate (other than where specified)

Northern Languedoc

Bellegarde and Costières de Nîmes

Costières means "gently sloping land", and the vineyards of Costières de Nîmes do indeed cover a low ridge of gently sloping hills, almost a plateau, south of historic Nîmes. To the east is the Rhône and to the west the vineyards of the sprawling Coteaux du Languedoc. The appellation's northern boundary runs along the A9 motorway, *La Languedoçienne*, just south of Nîmes. The canal linking the Rhône to the port of Sète and the marshy Camargue flats mark the southern border. This is good-value, red wine country with a pocket of characterful white Clairette around Bellegarde.

The low-lying Costières

This is a small appellation, just 40km by 15km (25 miles by 9 miles). The low-lying vineyards – they're between 20m and 100m (65–330 feet) in altitude – are distinguished by their complex, stony soils. There's sandy-chalk in the east, clay and chalk in the west, and a band of moisture-retaining clay a couple of metres (6.5 feet) below the surface throughout. The most important feature is the stony top layer with its distinctive red pebbles called *galets roulées*. The Rhône washed them down from the Alps and they're similar to those found in Châteauneuf-du-Pape. They force the vines' roots to dig deep while also reflecting light and heat.

This is one of the hottest areas in France, with temperatures only alleviated by the proximity of the Mediterranean and the Mistral, which can blow hard here. It doesn't rain often, but when it does it pours. Costières de Nîmes was granted AC status in 1986.

Travelling around

Relying on public transport is really not an option when visiting this region. Getting to Nîmes, however, is no problem. There are good train and airline services to the city from many parts. There are buses to towns around Nîmes too, but they're not a convenient way to visit *vignerons*. If you don't want to take the car, cycling is an option made all the more agreeable by the

LOCAL INFORMATION

Office de Tourisme
6 rue Auguste
30900 Nîmes
Tel: 04 66 58 38 01
www.ot-nimes.fr

BIKE HIRE: Cycles Rebour
38 rue Hôtel Dieu
30900 Nîmes
Tel: 04 66 76 24 92
Fax: 04 66 76 28 70
www.cycles-rebour.com

fairly flat terrain. Take plenty of water to drink in the summer when it can be extremely hot. Allow at least three days to explore Nîmes and the surrounding wine country.

Your tour will take in towns to the east of Nîmes as far as Beaucaire, at the junction of the Rhône and the Canal du Rhône à Sète. Beaucaire hosts a popular Latin American festival in July plus a lively summer festival – Estivales de Beaucaire – with a distinctly Camargais and Provençal feel (tel: 04 66 59 26 57). And between Beaucaire and Bellegarde, you will find both Château Mourges du Grès and Mas des Tourelles. Along the way, a detour via the town of Redessan will take you to the domaine of the same name.

The route to the south takes in towns on the way to St-Gilles, home of Château de la Tuilerie and Château Grande Cassagne, including Bouillargues and Bellegarde. St-Gilles, on the route of the pilgrimage of St-Jacques de Compostelle, is known as the gateway to the Camargue. It possesses one of the region's most remarkable works of medieval art, the

Costières de Nîmes
Three days is ample time to discover the city and surrounding wine country

Costières de Nîmes

Clairette de Bellegarde

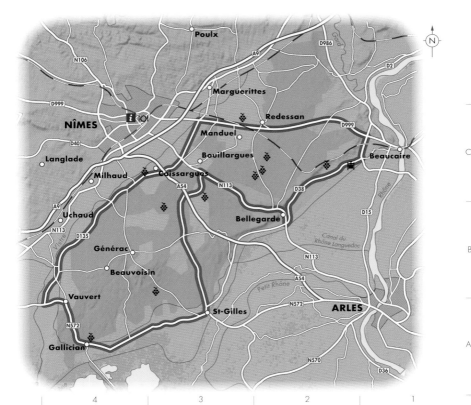

**GROWERS IN BELLET AND
COSTIERES DE NIMES**

Château de Belle Coste
30132 Caissargues
Tel: 04 66 20 26 48 *(C4)*

Château de Campuget
RD403, 30129 Manduel
Tel: 04 66 20 20 15 *(C3:
inexpensive to moderate)*

Château Grande Cassagne
30800 St-Gilles
Tel: 04 66 87 32 90 *(A3)*

Château de Mas Neuf
30600 Gallician
Tel: 04 66 73 33 23 *(A4)*

Château de Nages
30132 Caissargues
Tel: 04 66 38 44 33 *(C4:
inexpensive to moderate)*

Domaine du Mas Carlot
30127 Bellegarde
Tel: 04 66 01 11 83 *(C2:
moderate)*

Domaine du Vieux Relais
30129 Redessan
Tel: 04 66 20 07 69 *(C3)*

Mas des Bressades
30129 Manduel
Tel: 04 66 01 66 00 *(C3:
moderate)*

PRICES: *inexpensive* (other
than where specified)

Abbatiale, a twelfth-century Romanesque abbey church which is a UNESCO World Heritage monument St-Gilles also has a charming old town.

There are domaines like Château du Mas Neuf to be discovered west of St-Gilles around Gallician and Vauvert, and more are to be found on the route back to Nîmes via Générac and Milhaud.

A few minutes' drive north of Vauvert is the Perrier spring where the world's most famous water is bottled. A two-hour guided tour takes in the factory and the former Dr Perrier's mansion, now a museum (Les Bouillens, RN113, 30310 Vergèze, tel: 04 66 87 61 01).

What the wines are like
Costières de Nîmes is predominantly red wine country, with rosés accounting for about a quarter of production. The reds vary from the early drinking, light, and fruity style that you'd want to chill, to more dense reds that can be cellared for five or six years. The latter tend to include more Syrah and resemble Côtes du Rhône. The rosés are generally cheap and cheerful.

The area produces very little white wine, with some falling under the separate Clairette de Bellegarde appellation. This is a curious appellation within Costières de Nîmes. Given AC status in 1949, it never really took off and there are just a couple of independent producers plus the village cooperative. Good examples are lighter and more aromatic than the (Clairette-based, as you might guess) Clairette du Languedoc found to the north of Pézenas.

Although Costières de Nîmes is administratively part of the Rhône, the appellation's grape varieties have more in common with the neighbouring Coteaux du Languedoc. In recent years, the best domaines have ripped up the ubiquitous Carignan, which many say doesn't perform well here, and planted Syrah, Grenache, and some Mourvèdre, albeit with mixed results. Cinsault is not uncommon although it mostly goes into the rosés.

Plans for the whites
For whites, there are the usual Mediterranean varieties such as Grenache Blanc, Ugni Blanc, Clairette, and Maccabéo, plus the aromatic Roussanne and Marsanne from the northern Rhône. In general, the whites have yet to distinguish themselves and some producers are planting Viognier in the hope that it may one day be included in the appellation.

The wines, many of which come in the Nîmois bottle (resembling a Burgundy bottle), represent very good value for money. As elsewhere in the Midi, the best come from independent *vignerons* while many cooperatives turn out fairly indifferent plonk.

Top growers in Bellegarde and Costières de Nîmes (*see also* p.136)

Château Mourges du Grès
route de Bellegarde, 30300 Beaucaire,
tel: 04 66 59 46 10, mourguesdugres@wanadoo.fr
This large seventeenth-century *mas* is on the edge of the Costières plateau between Bellegarde and Beaucaire with views as far as Les Alpilles in Provence. The unpromising stony ground produces some of the best wines in the appellation. Owner François Collard did a stint at Château Lafite-Rothschild after oenology studies in Montpellier.

There are three ranges in all colours: the immediately accessible Galets, the superior Terre d'Argence, and the top Les Capitelles – named after the shepherd huts that dot the landscape. The red Les Capitelles is dominated by Syrah and represents very good value for money. (*C2: inexpensive*)

Château de la Tuilerie
route de St-Gilles, 30900 Nîmes, tel: 04 66 70 07 52,
vins@chateautuilerie.com, www.chateautuilerie.com
This beautifully renovated château close to Nîmes airport includes 300ha of fruit orchards and 70ha of vines. There's an impressive shop, too. Each *cuvée* comes in all three colours and they're very good; try the Cuvée Eole range, which includes white and rosé *vins de garde*.

The Sarments and Carte Blanche reds will please lovers of Syrah while the nearly pure, oak-aged Syrah Vieilles Vignes is

ABOVE *The Pont du Gard near Remoulins, a feat of Roman engineering. Each block of stone weighs six tonnes.*

WHERE TO STAY AND EAT

L'Ancien Théâtre
4 rue Racine
30900 Nîmes
Tel: 04 66 21 30 75

Imperator Concorde
quai de la Fontaine
30900 Nîmes
Tel: 04 66 21 90 30
Fax: 04 66 67 70 25
accueil@hotel-imperator.com
www.hotel-imperator.com

Le Lisita
2 blvd des Arènes
30900 Nîmes
Tel: 04 66 67 66 20
Fax: 04 66 76 22 30
restaurant site:
www.lelisita.com

Les Olivades
18 rue Jean-Reboul
30900 Nîmes
Tel: 04 66 21 71 78

RIGHT *Stone walls in the town of Les Matelles.*

BELOW *Horses at Prieuré de St-Jean-de-Bebian: the owner likes to ride through the vineyards.*

the top red. Prices are moderate, but look for the good value varietal *vins de pays*, including Cabernet, Viognier, and the new La Cascatelle Merlot. A star estate. (*B3: moderate*)

Mas des Tourelles
route de Bellegarde, 30300 Beaucaire,
tel: 04 66 59 19 72,
contact@tourelles.com, www.tourelles.com
They make wines the Roman way with pretty unusual ingredients at this sixteenth-century *mas* where in antiquity amphorae were manufactured. Carenum is Muscat with the addition of quince syrup, Turriculae includes Villard Blanc and iris rhizomes, whilst Mulsum is from Grenache Noir, honey, and spices. Take the tour and be the judge. More conventionally, a range of Costières wines is produced. The youthful Cuvée Classique is from Syrah and Grenache, La Cour des Glycines includes Mourvèdre and keeps for up to eight years, but the best is the oaked Grande Cuvée from old vines, mostly Syrah. It will keep for ten years. A fascinating place to visit, with well-made wines. (*C2: moderate*)

Two things to know about Nîmes
You'll notice the city's Philippe Starck-designed coat of arms. The mysterious crocodile chained to a palm tree commemorates the victory of Caesar's army over Mark Anthony and Cleopatra, and the conquest of Egypt. Veterans of the campaign were given land in Nîmes as a reward. The other thing you should know about the city is that it made a fortune from cotton. Levi Strauss bought cotton from here – the famous "denim" is derived from "de Nîmes".

Finding a place to stay
Staying in Nîmes allows you to discover the town's Roman past, modern architecture, and artistic life. There are lots of accommodation options. The best and most atmospheric hotel is the impeccable, four-star Imperator Concorde. The most desirable rooms in this *fin-de-siècle* mansion overlook the splendid garden. Alternatively, there's the reputable and characterful two-star Le Lisita, overlooking Les Arènes. This authentic town house has twenty-six comfortable rooms and a fine restaurant.

Eating out
Dining in Nîmes is a cosmopolitan experience. Spanish, Indian, and North African cuisine are much in evidence along with more traditional Mediterranean fare. The L'Ancien Théâtre near the Maison Carrée offers an inventive take on Mediterranean seafood with a continually renewed menu. The cosy Les Olivades near Les Arènes adjoins a *vinothèque* and has a good wine list and simple, local cuisine that's carefully prepared.

Pic St-Loup and Grès de Montpellier

The unfortunate St Loup was a hermit who lived on the Pic. He withdrew from the world after returning from a Crusade to discover that the object of his affections had left him. *C'est la vie*! Pic St-Loup is a Coteaux du Languedoc icon. One of the most recognizable landmarks in the appellation and one of the top *crus*, it's also a dynamic and compact area with a growing list of superior producers, many of them newcomers to the region. It will almost certainly become an AC in due course. The new Grès de Montpellier appellation includes three terroirs east of Pic St-Loup. They are St-Drézery, St-Christol, and Vérargues, each based around a village of the same name. Nearby are the famous sweet Muscats from Lunel.

Years of effort
For the moment, Pic St-Loup is a special *cru* within the Coteaux du Languedoc appellation. It earned *cru* standing in 1994 in recognition of its superior terroir and of efforts made in the previous decade by determined, quality-minded *vignerons*.

With *cru* status came stricter rules than before, in particular the requirement that Grenache, Mourvèdre, and Syrah make up ninety per cent of the red wine and that the vines be at least six years old. The *cru* applies to reds and rosés only; the latter may use grapes from younger vines.

St-Drézery, St-Christol, and Vérargues in the new Grès de Montpellier appellation are also currently classed as *crus* within the Coteaux du Languedoc (that patchy, catch-all AC scattered across the landscape from Narbonne to Nîmes). Vérargues has become something of a forgotten *cru* and its name is hardly used any more.

South of Vérargues and still within the Grès de Montpellier is the terroir of Muscat de Lunel. With just a handful of independent producers, the co-ops at Vérargues and Lunel dominate production of this old *vin doux naturel* appellation, granted AC status back in 1943.

What the wines are like
Pic St-Loup reds are well-balanced, sophisticated, full-bodied wines worthy of cellaring. Locals tell you it's because of the terroir. The soil is mainly clay and limestone, with stony debris giving way to more rocky soils on higher ground. The terroir is cooler

RIGHT *The Château de Notre Dame de Londres.*

GROWERS IN PIC ST-LOUP AND GRES

Château de Cazeneuve
34270 Lauret
Tel: 04 67 59 07 49 *(C3)*

Château de Lancyre
34270 Valflaunès
Tel: 04 67 55 32 74 *(C3: moderate)*

Château La Roque
34270 Fontanès
Tel: 04 67 55 34 47 *(C2: moderate to expensive)*

Clos Marie
34270 Lauret
Tel: 04 67 59 06 96 *(C3)*

Ermitage du Pic St-Loup
34270 St-Mathieu-de-Treviers
Tel: 04 67 55 20 15 *(B3: moderate to expensive)*

Mas Bruguière
34270 Valflaunès
Tel: 04 67 55 20 97 *(C4)*

Mas de Morties
34270 St-Jean-de-Cuculles
Tel: 04 67 55 11 12 *(B4) moderate)*

PRICES: *inexpensive to moderate (other than where specified)*

than elsewhere in the Languedoc, rainfall is higher than average and the wind from the north keeps temperatures from soaring and contributes to healthy grapes. The rosés tend to be full-bodied. The whites, although not classed as *cru* Pic St-Loup, are based on aromatic varieties like Roussanne, Rolle, and Viognier. They can be some of the best in the Midi.

Wines from St-Drézery, St-Christol, and Vérargues are generally lighter than those from Pic St-Loup and made for earlier drinking. Cooperatives play a bigger role here than in Pic St-Loup and there's just a handful of independent producers. Even taken together their output doesn't equal that of their neighbour to the west. Again, it's the independent *vignerons* of the Grès de Montpellier who make the most characterful, individual and robust wines.

A tour of the area should also take in the honey-sweet, white apéritif or dessert wines around Lunel, the historic capital of Muscat. The tiny appellation covers around 250ha. Napoleon, exiled on St-Helena, reportedly had his sister send him supplies of Muscat de Lunel.

Travelling around

A string of tiny villages and hamlets between St-Gély-du-Fesc in the south (A3) and Corconne, 20km (12 miles) to the north, makes up the entire Pic St-Loup appellation. The jagged, bare rock of Pic St-Loup, 658m (2,160-feet) high, and the cliffs of Montagne d'Hortus dominate these villages to the west.

To begin your exploration – and you'll want to allow yourself at least two days – head north from Montpellier, for 16km (10 miles) on the D17 into the *garrigue* and Pic St-Loup. The first producers, including Domaine de l'Hortus and Mas Bruguière, are west of St-Mathieu-de-Tréviers on a spectacular road leading to Château de Montferrand, one of the first castles to fall in the Cathar Crusades. Head back along the D17 north, passing Château de Lancyre and perhaps detouring via Lauret to see Château de Cazeneuve and Clos Marie, before reaching tiny Corconne beside the Montagne d'Hortus.

To visit the Grès de Montpellier vineyards head south via Vacquières, home of the ancient estate of Château de Lascaux, and St-Bauzille-de-Montmel, on the D107/D21. Producers are located around sleepy St-Drézéry and the wine village of St-Christol, where you will find Château des Hospitaliers and Domaine de la Coste. The route takes in handsome Sommières, adopted hometown of Lawrence Durrell, and a number of producers around Fontanès and Aspères. Visiting Pic St-Loup and Grès de Montpellier producers by bicycle is an option. The domaines are not far from each other in both appellations and the terrain is fairly undemanding, with minor roads connecting most villages. The land is particularly flat around Lunel where vineyards are on average 60m (200 feet) in altitude.

Top growers in Pic St-Loup and Grès de Montpellier

Château de Lascaux

place de l'Eglise, 34270 Vacquières, tel: 04 67 59 00 08, info@chateau-lascaux.com, www.chateau-lascaux.com
Another star, this estate in the stony, *garrigue*-covered Cévennes foothills has been in the same family for 800 years. There are two whites, two reds, and a rosé. The basic white Cuvée

LOCAL INFORMATION AND WHERE TO STAY

Office de Tourisme
16 cours Gabriel Péri
34402 Lunel
Tel: 04 67 71 01 37
Fax: 04 67 71 26 67
otlunel@capline.fr
www.lunel.com

Auberge du Cèdre,
Domaine de Cazeneuve
34270 Lauret
Tel: 04 67 59 02 02

Château de Boisseron
34160 Boisseron
Tel: 04 67 87 47 70

Pic St-Loup

Grès de Montpellier

Spend a couple of days discovering this wine country

Coteaux de Languedoc

Muscat

0   5 Km
0   5 miles

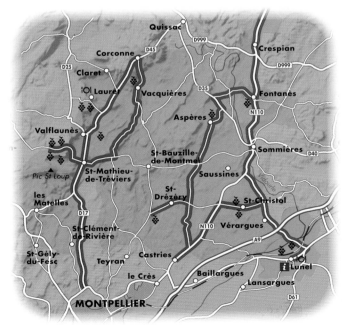

GROWERS CONTINUED

. . . .

Château Grès St-Paul
route de Restinclières
34400 Lunel
Tel: 04 67 71 27 90
This estate, with its
Italianate château, is a
good place to shop for
sweet Muscats, like the
Sevillane, and spicy reds,
like the oak-aged Antonin
and Sirius. *(A1: moderate)*

Château des Hospitaliers
Domaine Martin-Pierrat
1 rue des Chardonnerets
34400 St-Christol
Tel: 04 67 86 01 15
This attractive former
property of the Knights
of Malta produces
superior whites featuring
Marsanne, Roussanne and
Chardonnay. Don't miss
an opportunity to try the
Prestige and Réserve
reds, too. *(B2: inexpensive)*

Mas de Bellevue
route de Sommières
34400 Lunel
Tel: 04 67 83 24 83
Buy the stunning Clos
Bellevue from this supplier
of superior Muscats to the
Elysée Palace. There's also
a late-harvested Muscat
Fût de Chêne made
in exceptional years
from miniscule yields.
(A1: moderate to expensive)

Mas Montel
30250 Aspères
Tel: 04 66 80 01 21
Hundred-year-old giant oak
foudres are still used at this
former farm of the Abbaye
de Psalmodi in Aigues-
Mortes. Buy the white Les
Marnes plus the Tradition
and Les Grès reds.
(C2: moderate)

Classique is from Marsanne, Roussanne, Rolle, and Viognier. The superior Les Pierres d'Argent includes more Viognier and some wood. The basic red is a spicy Syrah and Grenache while the top Les Nobles Pierres is nearly pure Syrah and oak-aged, with great finesse and ageing potential. *(B3: moderate)*

Château Puech-Haut
2250 route de Teyran, 34160 St-Drézery,
tel: 04 67 86 59 23, chateau.puech-haut@wanadoo.fr
This eighteenth-century country mansion used to be a wing of the Montpellier prefecture. Puech-Haut's irrepressible owner, Gérard Bru, had it dismantled, transported and reconstructed on a new site. He also built the ultra-modern *cave* and over ten years created the 100ha vineyard out of the gently rolling local *garrigue*. Today, this estate is a benchmark for other producers even though the wines are not always representative of the appellation. All Puech-Haut wines get the oak treatment. The complex Roussanne, Marsanne, and Viognier blend is inspired by the northern Rhône. The red Tête de Cuvée is a potent Syrah and old Carignan *vin de garde*. Deservedly expensive. *(B2)*

Domaine de l'Hortus
route de St-Martin de Londres, 34270 Valflaunès,
tel: 04 67 55 31 20
Jean Orliac is a star of the region who turned abandoned terraces between Pic St-Loup and the Montagne d'Hortus into premium vineyards. He has Mourvèdre on south-facing slopes, Syrah on the northern slopes and some Grenache and white varieties lower down in the valley. He makes two ranges in white and red: the basic Bergerie de l'Hortus and the superior Domaine de l'Hortus Grande Cuvée. Both whites are *vins de pays* as they use non-appellation varieties. The Chardonnay and Viognier Grande Cuvée is arguably the best white in the Languedoc. The red Grande Cuvée is perhaps the best red in the appellation. *(B4: moderate to expensive)*

Finding a place to stay

There's lots of accommodation in nearby Montpellier, but consider the idyllic Auberge du Cèdre outside Lauret. This ex-wine domaine's *maison de maître* has nineteen cosy rooms, Mediterranean cuisine and occasional gourmet evenings (open from mid-March to the end of November).

Château de Boisseron, just south of Sommières in the heart of the Grès de Montpellier, has thirty-five comfortable rooms surrounded by parkland, and is ideally placed for a tour around St-Drézery, St-Christol, and Vérargues.

If you're dining in the area, try the L'Authentic in Lunel for some distinctively Camarguais décor and cuisine.

St-Georges-d'Orques and Picpoul de Pinet

S t-Georges-d'Orques is a small Coteaux du Languedoc *cru* with a long reputation and distinguished admirers, including Thomas Jefferson, one-time American ambassador to France. The *cru* is one of the western terroirs in the Grès de Montpellier appellation and has a strong sense of its identity. Nearby Picpoul de Pinet is a compact, fashionable Coteaux de Languedoc *cru* that merits appellation status. It should be only a matter of time before this happens. It already has its own distinctive, slender "Neptune" bottle. Between the two *crus* are the sweet Muscats of Mireval and Frontignan.

Wine with a long history

Picpoul de Pinet is the only white Coteaux du Languedoc *cru*. It was recognized by the wine authorities in 1946 and made a *cru* in 1985. The earliest records extolling its virtues date from 1600, while the grape variety on which it's based is mentioned in medieval texts. Picpoul de Pinet's distinctiveness is summarized by the appellation's slogan: "its terroir is the sea", and from the fact that it's made from just a single grape variety, the Picpoul.

The origin of the curious "St-Georges-d'Orques" name is something of a mystery but the wines have a long recorded history. They were exported around the world in the 1600s and for a long time were better known than Burgundy's Nuits St-Georges. Today, there are lots of independent producers and the cooperative no longer dominates production. The only threat to the appellation appears to be the encroachment of the nearby Montpellier suburbs.

Mireval, on the Etang de Vic lagoon (C4), and Frontignan, on the Etang d'Ingril, are south of Montpellier between the Montagne de la Gardiole and the sea. The towns give their names to their respective sweet Muscats. The Muscats of Frontignan have a long and illustrious reputation. Thomas Jefferson, always the busy ambassador, certainly enjoyed them. The Muscats of Mireval were so admired by Rabelais that they named their cooperative after him.

BELOW *Take a break from wine and the sun to explore the striking architecure of this area.*

Travelling around

Plan to spend at least two days exploring the wine country and longer if you plan to discover Montpellier. Check out Château de Flaugergues (*see* right) as you begin your trip from Montpellier. Heading west, it's not long before you're on gently undulating land in the heart of St-Georges d'Orques territory. Begin with the historic Châteaux of Engarron and Fourques near Juvignac and Lavérune (*D4*), before venturing out to Pignan to see Domaine Icard. Then head to St-Georges d'Orques itself for Domaine Henry. For the sweeties of Mireval and Frontignan, join the N112 which follows the Etang de Vic south. After taking in domaines in Muscat territory, visit the charming port of Sète, set on a hill overlooking the Etang de Thau and the sea.

The Picpoul de Pinet vineyards are further along the coast between Pézenas and Agde, with producers concentrated around the villages of Pinet, Mèze, Castelnau-de-Guers,

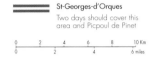

St-Georges-d'Orques
Two days should cover this area and Picpoul de Pinet

0   2   4   6   8   10 Km
0   2   4   6 miles

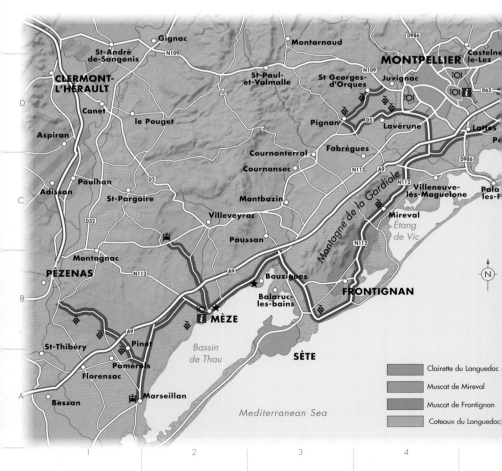

Montagnac, and Pomérols. Heading southwest from Mèze, visit Domaine Félines-Jourdan, before making for the village of Pinet to see Domaine du Petit Roubie and Caveau Gaujal.

If you want to leave the car at home, cycling around Montpellier and out to St-Georges-d'Orques is an option (*see* below for rentals). Montpellier itself boasts 120km (75 miles) of cycle paths. The fairly flat terrain around the Picpoul vineyards makes cycling a good option here too. Bike hire is available in Le Cap d'Agde. Or you can easily take the train from Montpellier to Agde, and begin exploring the Picpoul de Pinet vineyards from there, stopping in Mireval and Frontignan on the way to sample the Muscats.

ABOVE *A detail of a chair in the Château de l'Engarran museum (see p.86).*

What the wines are like

According to local *vignerons*, it's primarily the soil that gives the wines of St-Georges-d'Orques their elegance and balance. Rising to 150m (490 feet) in altitude, the soil is deep, chalky clay with pebbly terraces around Murveil and iron-rich, red limestone and gravel elsewhere. The Muscats of Frontignan and Mireval have much in common. They're both supposed to be based on the same variety of Muscat (Muscat à Petits Grains, the best and most elegant strain of the grape), they taste alike and the vineyards of both appellations are just inland on distinctive, white chalky soils. The only reason they're not part of the same appellation is their desire to be seen as separate.

In Picpoul de Pinet, the wine is based solely on the Picpoul grape which thrives in the area's gravelly limestone and sandy-clay soil. Vineyards are on gentle slopes that rise to just 50m (164 feet) in altitude and extend a few kilometres inland towards Pézenas from the banks of the Bassin de Thau, one of the biggest salt-water lagoons in the Languedoc. Maritime influences are significant here and the vineyards benefit from cooling sea breezes.

Picpoul de Pinet has developed a reputation as the perfect accompaniment to the oysters and mussels cultivated in the Bassin de Thau. The wine's lemony tang provides a refreshing note of acidity that perfectly complements the bivalves.

Top growers in St-Georges d'Orques

Château de l'Engarran

34880 Lavérune, tel: 04 67 47 00 02, contact@chateau-engarran.com, www.chateau-engarran.com
There's a small wine museum at this eighteenth-century château-folly set in elegant French gardens just outside Montpellier. It's one of several follies from the period. Uncommonly, the winemakers are all women here, a tradition going back three generations. Predictably their wines are often described as "feminine". Perhaps "Rubenesque" gets closer to the truth. The

GROWERS IN ST-GEORGES-D'ORQUES

Château de Flaugergues
1744 ave Albert Einstein
34000 Montpellier
Tel: 04 99 52 66 37
Visit this elegant château-folly for the staircase alone with its bright Flemish tapestries, then buy the easy-drinking "Sélection" or the top red *cuvée* Constance. (*B4: moderate*)

Château de Fourques
route de Lavérune
34990 Juvignac
Tel: 04 67 47 90 87
You'll find a range of inexpensive St-Georges-d'Orques reds at Château l'Engarran's neighbour. Try the rosé based on the now uncommon Aramon, too. (*B4:inexpensive*)

Domaine Icard
route de St-Georges-d'Orques, 34570 Pignan
Tel: 04 67 75 31 31
The Icard family have been in Pignan since before the Revolution and produce a simple range of good-value St-Georges-d'Orques reds. (*D3: inexpensive*)

LOCAL INFORMATION AND WHERE TO STAY AND EAT

Office de Tourism
place de la Comedie
34000 Montpellier
Tel: 04 67 60 60 60
Fax: 04 67 60 60 61
www.ot-montpellier.fr

Office de Tourisme
8 rue Massaloup
34140 Mèze
Tel: 04 67 43 93 08
Fax: 04 67 43 55 61
www.ville-meze.fr

BIKE HIRE: Vill'a Vélo
27 rue Maguelone
34000 Montpellier
Tel: 04 67 22 87 82

Cyclo du Mail
La Palme d'Or
27 mail de Rochelongue
34300 Le Cap d'Agde
Tel: 04 67 26 90 61

Château de Bionne
1225 rue Bionne
34070 Montpellier
Tel: 04 67 45 20 93
Fax: 04 67 45 71 52
contact@chateau-bionne.com
www.chateau-bionne.com

Le Jardin des Sens
11 ave St-Lazare
34000 Montpellier
Tel: 04 99 58 38 38
Fax: 04 99 58 38 39
www.jardindessens.com

Tripti Kulai
20 rue Jacques-Coeur
34000 Montpellier
Tel: 04 67 66 30 51
One for vegetarians.

RIGHT *The picture-postcard port of Sète.*

top Cuvée Quetton is round, ripe and very substantial, not lacking in finesse either. It's dominated by old Syrah and part-aged in oak. On a lighter note, there's a wonderfully aromatic pure domaine Sauvignon Blanc *vin de pays*. (*D4: moderate*)

Domaine Henry
ave d'Occitanie, 34680 St-Georges-d'Orques,
tel: 04 67 45 57 74, domainehenry@wanadoo.fr,
www.domainehenry.fr
There are more than ten generations of winemaking experience behind this relative newcomer to the area. The Henrys made their first wines here as recently as 1993. But there are old vines in the vineyards, including some eighty-year-old Cinsault. One of the newest *cuvées* is based on some very old and long-forgotten varieties: Aspiran Noir, Morastel, and Oeillade. The Coteaux range includes the easy-drinking Paradines and the upmarket St-Georges *cuvées*. These are wines of considerable finesse. Look for the sweet, late-harvested Passerillé from Grenache. Buy it if you're feeling flush. Make an appointment. (*D3: moderate to expensive*)

Abbaye de Valmagne
34560 Villeveyrac, tel: 04 67 78 06 09,
valmagne@valmagne.com, www.valmagne.com
This twelfth-century Cistercian abbey was one of the richest in the south of France for several hundred years, and it shows. The abbey's gothic church, unusual for the Midi, contains some 200-year-old *foudres*. The cloisters, chapter house and fountain garden are charming. The medieval garden contains medicinal plants while there's a pedagogical path around the grape conservatory. The wines are great value. Buy the white Roussanne and Viognier Cuvée Turenne and the red version, from Syrah and Mourvèdre. And try the white Nonenque, almost pure Viognier. The red version contains the rare Morrastel, and both are *vins de pays*. The estate is outside the St-Georges terroir, east of Pézenas. (*B2:inexpensive to moderate*)

Finding a place to stay
The seventeenth-century Château de Bionne on the western edge of Montpellier is an ideal spot to base yourself for exploring St-Georges-d'Orques. The twenty-nine suites are in an attractive, modern annex set in 5ha of parkland. The château's gourmet restaurant, Le Grand Arbre, is highly recommended. Just a few kilometres away are the châteaux and domaines of St-Georges-d'Orques.

There are a huge number and variety of restaurants in Montpellier, too. The universally acclaimed Le Jardin des Sens is perhaps the best in the Languedoc.

Mèze is a good place to find restaurants serving the local shellfish. Wander down the waterfront quai Descournut and check out Le Chabichou or Le Coquillou and others. Alternatively, in Agde (along the coast further south) look for restaurants along the quayside on rue Chassefière. Between Agde and the old fishing village of La Grau d'Agde on the river Hérault is the gastronomic La Tramissière, one of the best restaurants in the area.

Other things to do

Guided tours of Montpellier take in the city's Renaissance mansions, the old town and some sights normally closed to visitors (the tourist office has details, see left). Highlights include the Musée Fabré (tel: 04 67 14 83 00) with its collection of eighteenth- and nineteenth-century French art. In Marseillan, the biggest attraction is the Noilly Prat cellars (tel: 04 67 77 20 15). There's a museum in Bouzigues about the Etang de Thau (tel: 04 67 78 33 57). Agde also has a good museum about the area, the Musée Agathois (tel: 04 67 94 82 51). The star of Cap d'Adge's Musée de l'Ephèbe (tel: 04 67 94 69 60) is the Hellenistic bronze statuette, the Ephèbe d'Agde. There's also an aquarium in Cap d'Adge (tel: 04 67 26 14 21). Mèze has a dinosaur park-museum (tel: 04 67 43 02 80) and an eco-park (tel: 04 67 46 64 80, open June to October). Nearby Balaruc-le-Vieux is an ancient fishing village with medieval walls and an eleventh-century church. Sète is worth a visit too.

GROWERS IN PICPOUL DE PINET

Domaine Félines-Jourdan
34140 Mèze
Tel: 04 67 43 69 29
The Jourdans' Picpoul is bigger and fruitier than most. They also make an attractive late-harvested, slightly oaked Muscat. *(B2: inexpensive)*

Domaine de la Grangette
34120 Castlenau-de-Guers
Tel: 04 67 98 13 56
Buy the floral L'Enfant Terrible and the oaked La Part des Anges from this organic domaine run by Rioja ex-pats. *(B1: inexpensive)*

Domaine du Petit Roubié
34850 Pinet
Tel: 04 67 77 09 28
The top Picpoul is the Arbre Blanc at this highly commendable producer of characterful organic wines. Look for the Arbre Rouge too. *(B1: inexpensive)*

Pézenas, Cabrières, and Les Terrasses du Larzac

The Pézenas and Cabrières *crus* are directly east of Faugères. Cabrières contains one of the oldest white wine appellations in the Languedoc, Clairette du Languedoc. The St-Saturnin and Montpeyroux vineyards are part of the Terrasses du Larzac, north of Clermont-l'Hérault and near the river Hérault. These are the Languedoc's most northerly vineyards. The countryside north of Pézenas is dotted with villages and gets wilder and hillier as you head to the mountains of the Cévennes and the edge of the Languedoc. You can use Pézenas as your point of departure. This elegant town is the best example of Languedoc's "Golden Age" and well worth exploring.

BELOW *The thin streets of the village of Castelneu de Guers.*

Travelling around

You'll want to stay for at least two days to explore the wine country and longer to take in the delights of Pézenas. The Pézenas and Cabrières vineyards fan out north from Pézenas to Aspiran and west to Gabian. The Terrasses du Larzac are northeast of Clermont-l'Hérault with producers concentrated around the tiny villages of St-André-de-Sangonis, St-Saturnin-de-Lucian, Montpeyroux, and Aniane.

Begin this wine route by heading north or west from Pézenas towards Aspiran or Roujan respectively. In between, country roads criss-cross vine-covered valleys and take in the wine villages of Caux, Fontès, and Neffiès, with its thirteenth-century gothic church and panoramic views over the Cabrières wine country.

A visit to Cabrières should include a detour to the village's copper mines, exploited since Neolithic times (guided tours from April to November; tel: 04 67 39 03 18). The circular village of Paulhan, with its steep, narrow streets and ancient houses, some dating from the fifteenth century, is worth a visit too (leave the car outside the village centre).

Roujan is the centre of the area's viticultural life and notable for its twelfth-century church of St-Laurent. Head north, beyond quiet Clermont-l'Hérault, to reach producers across Les Terrasses de Larzac where the wine route, dominated by the mountains of the Cévennes,

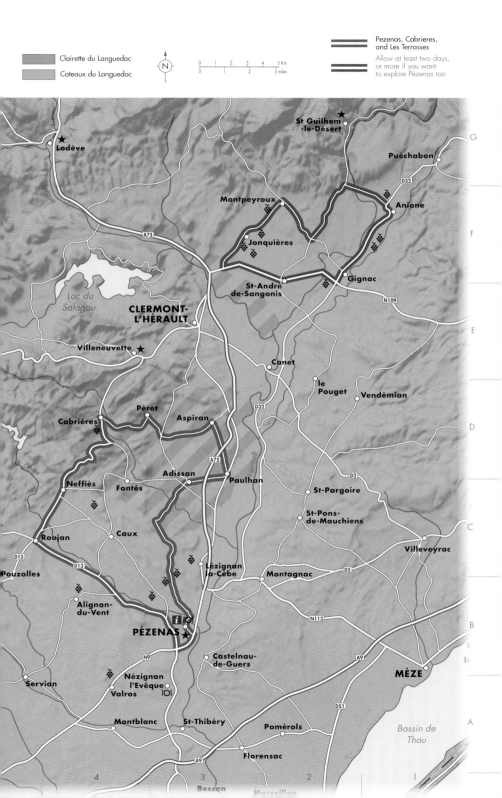

Clairette du Languedoc

Coteaux du Languedoc

N

0 1 2 3 4 5 Km
0 1 2 3 miles

Pezenas, Cabrieres, and Les Terrasses

Allow at least two days, or more if you want to explore Pézenas too

takes in the wine villages of St-André-de-Sangonis (visit Château de Granoupiac), Gignac, Aniane, Montpeyroux, and Jonquières. Of these, Aniane is home to Château Capion, Domaine de la Soranne, and the peerless Mas de Daumas-Gassac, while Jonquières, not to be outdone, boasts the biodynamic estate, Mas Jullien, and the eponymous château. East of the Terrasses du Larzac is the artificial Lac Salagou, surrounded by striking red, iron-rich soils; the eerie Cirque de Mourèze, a forest of weirdly eroded 160-million-year-old dolomites (some reaching 100m/328 feet high), is just south of Lac Salagou – it's the most important site of its kind in France.

Appellations and *crus*

Some of the top *vignerons* in Pézenas and Cabrières are newcomers to the area, although the two terroirs have a long history. Pink wines have been made in Cabrières since the middle ages and the village was one of the original Coteaux du Languedoc *crus*. Cabrières now looks set to be absorbed into the putative appellation of Pézenas. However, Cabrières producers would like to preserve their separate identity rather than be part of a broader Pézenas terroir.

There is just a handful of Clairette du Languedoc producers. The appellation is being revived by a number of *vignerons* who believe it should be more than a local curiosity. There are many old Clairette vines in the area and judicious vinification demonstrates why some producers feel so strongly that the appellation should not be forgotten.

St-Saturnin and Montpeyroux are adjoining Coteaux du Languedoc *crus* in the Terraces du Larzac terroir north of Cabrières, in wild, hilly and sparsely populated countryside. St-Saturnin is dominated to the north by the Rocher des Vierges (539m/1,768 feet) and nearby Montpeyroux looks straight at Mont St-Baudille (848m/2,782 feet).

What the wines are like

The best domaines in Pézenas are in the hills to the north, towards the *cru* of Cabrières (C4). Here wines in all three colours are produced according to Coteaux du Languedoc regulations. Neighbouring Cabrières is surrounded by hills and dominated by Pic de Vissou (480m/1,575 feet). The vineyards occupy the southeast-facing slopes that descend towards the river Hérault. Long ago, Cabrières established a reputation for deeply coloured, Cinsault-based rosés, although reds and Clairette-based whites are more important today.

The authorities never laid down rules governing the vinification of Clairette du Languedoc, so there are many styles. A sweet version has become increasingly popular though more common is a dry, fruity white somewhat more substantial

GROWERS IN PEZENAS

Château la Condamine-Bertrand
34230 Paulhan
Tel: 04 67 25 27 96 *(C3)*

Château de Montpezat
34120 Pézenas
Tel: 04 67 98 10 84 *(B3)*

Château St-André
34120 Pézenas
Tel: 04 67 98 33 46 *(B3: inexpensive to moderate)*

Domaine Deshenrys
34290 Alignan-du-Vent
Tel: 04 67 24 91 67 *(B4)*

Domaine Fontedicto
34720 Caux
Tel: 04 67 98 40 22 *(C4)*

Domaine Montrose
34120 Pézenas
Tel: 04 67 98 63 33 *(B4: inexpensive)*

Domaine du Temple
34800 Cabrières
Tel: 04 67 96 02 48 *(D4: inexpensive)*

PRICES: *moderate (other than where specified)*

than Clairette de Bellegarde, from south of Nîmes. There are old Clairette vines in Cabrières and a small number of outstanding producers who are bringing dignity back to this ancient, sometimes maligned appellation.

St-Saturnin is dominated by two village cooperatives and has developed a reputation for its *vin de primeur* and *rosé d'une nuit*. The former is a fruity, young red that's more substantial than other *primeurs* while the latter is more of a light red than a rosé – the name derives from the short time it spends on the skins. Both are from Grenache, Cinsault, and Syrah, with Carignan included in the rosé.

Montpeyroux has a greater number of independent *vignerons* than its neighbour and has made impressive progress in the last five to ten years. It is now internationally recognized for its rich and full red *vins de garde*.

Top grower in Pézenas
La Prieuré de St-Jean-de-Bébian
route de Nizas, 34120 Pézenas, tel: 04 67 98 13 60, info@bebian.com, www.bebian.com

The former editor of the French wine magazine *Revue du Vin de France*, Chantal Lecouty, runs this colourfully restored property with fellow former wine journalist, Jean-Claude Lebrun. The secret of her wines is twofold: very low-yields and very ripe fruit. Grapes are also sorted meticulously and each variety is vinified separately. The property has seventeenth-century stone vats for long, slow macerations. The wines match their Rolls-Royce

LEFT *A gothic doorway in Pézenas.*

BELOW *Waterlogged vines near Pézenas: not the best thing for quality.*

GROWERS IN THE TERRASSES DU LARZAC

Château Capion
34150 Aniane
Tel: 04 67 57 71 37
Vins de pays from single varieties and blends of Bordelais and Midi varieties. Buy the top red Le Juge and Le Sorbier Chardonnay. *(F1: moderate)*

Château de Granoupiac
34725 St-André-de-Sangonis
Tel: 04 67 57 58 28
Claude Flavard still uses foudres that go back to the nineteenth-century origins of the château. Buy his red Garance for everyday. *(E2: inexpensive to moderate)*

Château de Jonquières
34725 Jonquières
Tel: 04 67 96 62 58
Look for the Risée de Blanc from old-vine Clairette at this fabulous estate. Buy the unusual, barrel-fermented Comte de Lansade white, too. *Chambres d'hôtes* available. *(F3: moderate)*

Domaine d'Auphilhac
28 rue du Plô
34150 Montpeyroux
Tel: 04 67 96 61 19
The energetic Sylvain Fadat makes a sensational old-vine Carignan. Also buy his superb red Montpeyroux, Le Clos. Afternoon visits only. *(F2: expensive)*

Domaine de la Seranne
route de Puéchabon
34150 Aniane
Tel: 04 67 57 37 99
Buy the superior rosé Sous les Micocouliers, the white Aventure, and the award-winning red, Le Clos des Immortelles from young *vigneron* Jean-Pierre Venture. *(F1: moderate)*

reputation. Economize with the La Chapelle range or shell out on the Le Prieuré in red or white. These are rich and expressive wines, but also expensive. *(B3)*

Top growers in Les Terrasses *(see also p.136)*

Mas de Daumas-Gassac

34150 Aniane, tel: 04 67 57 71 28,
prives@daumas-gassac.com, www.daumas-gassac.com
A leading Languedoc estate with over thirty varietals. The top wines don't come cheap but are deservedly called *grands crus*. These are the Mas de Daumas-Gassac wines. Moulin de Gassac is the budget range. The wines' character comes from the unique red, powdery soils and the emphasis on Cabernet Sauvignon. The owner of this estate famously led opposition to Californian winemaker Robert Mondavi's plans to move into the area. All wines are *vins de pays*. *(F1: moderate to expensive)*

Mas Jullien

route de St-André, 34725 Jonquières, tel: 04 67 96 60 04
Olivier Jullien is a Montpeyroux star and a leading young Languedoc independent. His Biodynamic wines are original, uncompromising and extremely good value. Buy the superb white Les Vignes Oubliées that includes two almost forgotten varieties: Carignan Blanc and Terret Blanc. And buy the peachy Viognier, Chenin and Grenache Blanc La Méjanne. Take home a case of red Les Etats d'Ame for everyday, quality drinking and buy the Les Cailloutis or Les Depierres *vins de garde* if you can find them. The first is a classic Midi blend; the second is a blend from selected vineyard parcels. *(F2: moderate to expensive)*

Finding a place to stay

Pézenas is a good place to base yourself when exploring the northern Languedoc wine country. It's the last decent-sized settlement on the Hérault as you head towards the Cévennes.

It's also a very beautiful town, noted for its fine architecture and cultural life. The sixteenth and seventeenth centuries were its heyday, the most famous resident being Molière, attracted here by the patronage of Armand de Bourbon, governor of Languedoc. Clive of India also holidayed here and bequeathed to the town a recipe for a spicy Indian meat pie, still a local speciality. The town boasts some fine museums and magnificent *hôtels particulières* or private mansions. The countryside around Pézenas offers lots of options for walkers and cyclists.

There are half a dozen or so hotels in and around Pézenas. The two-star Le Molière in Pézenas has sixteen rooms and a decent restaurant. Just south of Pézenas in quiet Nézignan L'Evêque is the three-star, nineteenth-century Hostellerie de St-Alban, set among vines, with thirteen rooms, a pool and a good restaurant. Dining out should include a meal at Le Mimosa in St-Guiraud, just outside St-Félix-de-Lodez. The restaurant is in an eighteenth-century *vigneron's* house and is popular with those in the know in Montpellier. There's an excellent wine list and an emphasis on organic, local produce prepared with Mediterranean style.

Other things to do

Château de Cassan, 2km (1.2 miles) west of Roujan, originally founded by Charlemagne, was rebuilt in the seventeenth century as a huge, neoclassical palace. There's a Romanesque church, an immense cloister with a fine iron staircase, the remains of a medieval hospital, plus an Oriental garden founded by Armand de Bourbon, the Languedoc's governor at the time (tel: 04 67 24 87 60). The medieval UNESCO World Heritage Site of St-Guilhem-le-Désert is 7km (4 miles) north of Aniane. The nearby cave, the Grotte de Clamouse, is one of the top tourist attractions in the Hérault (*G2*: tel: 04 67 57 71 05).

There's not much to detain you in Aniane itself, except the Baroque St-Sauveur church and the dynamic cooperative. Livelier is the nearby market town of Gignac. A few kilometres west of Clermont-L'Hérault is Villeneuvette, a charming old purpose-built textile mill town now turned over to artisans and artists. Lodève, another former cloth town, is rather remote but worth a detour for its impressive Gothic St-Fulcran cathedral and the Musée Fleury (tel: 04 67 88 86 10), which contains fine arts and archaeological finds, including dinosaur bones and Gallo-Roman artefacts. The town is today rather unromantically the capital of French uranium mining.

WHERE TO STAY AND EAT

Hostellerie de St-Alban
31 route d'Agde
34120 Nézignan l'Evêque
Tel: 04 67 98 11 38

Le Mimosa
Grand Rue
34725 St-Guiraud
Tel: 04 67 96 67 96
Fax: 04 67 96 61 15

Le Molière
place de 14 Juillet
34120 Pézenas
Tel: 04 67 98 14 00

LEFT *Geese in the vines: they provide natural fertiliser.*

BELOW *The town of Pézenas, worth a visit for its architecture and cultural life.*

Faugères

. . . .

The Faugères *cru* spread out across the schistous hills north and west of historic Béziers. It is sandwiched between Minervois country to the west and the vineyards of Pézenas to the east. This is rugged, desolate, beautiful countryside offering spectacular views across the plain to Béziers and the Mediterranean.

Coteaux *cru*

Faugères was originally an appellation in its own right; it became a *cru* of the Coteaux du Languedoc when the departmental appellation was created in 1985. The vineyards are set in the *garrigue*-covered foothills of the Cévennes just 25km (15 miles) north of Béziers. The terroir straddles the D909 south of the Orb Valley and includes just a handful of tiny hamlets linked by winding country lanes. The vineyards themselves cover terraces and slopes between 150 and 400m (490 and 1,300 feet) in altitude.

Travelling around

The D909 out of Béziers heads straight for Faugères. A good place to get an overview of the Faugères vineyards is the hill above the town, where three Roman towers (converted into windmills in the seventeenth century) dot the summit. They are the symbol of the appellation.

BELOW *Windmills are the symbol of the Faugères region.*

The first producer to visit, Domaine La Colombette, is just 5km (3 miles) north of Béziers on the D909, technically outside the Faugères terroir. Continue north and you pass the perched town of Magalas and the Oppidum of Montfo, both worth a detour (*A2*). Alternatively, take the D154 out of Béziers to picturesque Murviel-lès-Béziers, an almond-shaped "circular" village overlooking the Orb Valley with a gothic church and medieval château. Laurens, between Magalas and sleepy Faugères, is a tiny, formerly fortified village and gateway to the isolated estate of Château Grézan, a sort of mini-Aigues-Mortes.

The wine route's other attraction is tiny Cabrerolles, gateway to a number of interesting wineries, including the Domaine du Météore. Travelling south, the hamlet of La Liquière is home to the château of the same name, and Domaine St-Antonin, while the next little village, Lentheric, counts the pioneering Domaine Léon Barral as one of its own. Finally, you will reach Château Moulin de Ciffre at Autignac.

What the wines are like

Faugères has around forty independent *vignerons*, many relatively young, and three cooperatives (Faugères, Laurens, and Autignac) producing firm, full, characterful, *garrigue*-scented, red *vins de garde* and rosés with mineral notes from the predominantly schist soil. For the moment, there is no Faugères white wine, although trials are underway with Muscat, Viognier, Marsanne, and Roussanne with a view to appellation status.

Top growers in Faugères (*see also p.136*)

Château Moulin de Ciffre

34480 Autignac, tel: 04 67 90 11 45, info@moulindeciffre.com, www.moulindeciffre.com

It took Bernadette and Jacques Lesineau two years to find Château Moulin de Ciffre after leaving Bordeaux in search of the right Languedoc property. The restored mill is beside the river Taurou in an idyllic valley setting surrounded by vineyards and garrigue west of Autignac. There's a mosaic of terroirs at this junction of Faugères and St-Chinian with the usual ensemble

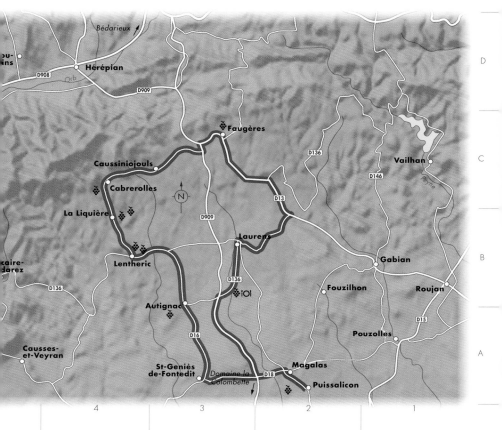

ABOVE *Mont Caroux (see p.98); dramatic and rugged.*

of Midi grapes, plus Cabernet and Viognier. There's a subtly oaked version of the latter while the Val Taurou includes the former. The top wines are Faugères. The Cuvée Eole is the star *vin de garde*. But for fruit without the oak, buy the basic St-Chinian. (*B3: moderate to expensive*)

Domaine La Colombette
Ancienne route de Bedarieux, 34500 Béziers,
tel: 04 67 31 05 53
This domaine 5km (3 miles) north of Béziers is outside the appellation so instead produces *vins de pays* of extraordinary quality and character. The domaine first made a name for itself on the back of a world-class Chardonnay. Other varietals make up this good-value range, including a zesty Sauvignon, a superior Pinot Noir rosé, a remarkable red Lladoner Pelut aged in 600-litre barrels and an outstanding Pinot Noir red. There are two blended reds from Syrah, Grenache, and Cabernet, one oaked. Buy as much as you can carry. (*see* A3: *inexpensive to expensive*)

Domaine Léon Barral
Hameau de Lenthéric, 34480 Cabrerolles,
tel: 04 67 90 29 13
Didier Barral is a young, independent-minded *vigneron* who withdrew from the local co-op to make his own wines when he took over his father's domaine. According to Barral, wines are made in the vineyard with the simplest of vinifications in the *cave*. His vines are organic and he eschews cultured yeasts.

WHERE TO STAY AND EAT
. . . .
L'Ambassade
22 Blvd de Verdun
34500 Béziers
Tel: 04 67 76 06 24

La Framboisier
12 rue Boieldieu
34500 Béziers
Tel: 04 67 49 90 00

Hôtel Imperator
28 Allées Paul Riquet
34500 Béziers
Tel: 04 67 49 02 25
www.hotel-imperator.fr

Hôtel des Poètes
80 Allées Paul Riquet
34500 Béziers
Tel: 04 67 76 38 66

His wines have an unmatched depth of colour and concentration of fruit with well-integrated oak. The Cuvée Jardis spends two years in barrels, and the top Cuvée Valinière is based on his beloved Mourvèdre.

These wines don't come cheap and they're hard to find. Buy them and economize on wher you stay. (*C4: moderate to expensive*)

Finding a place to stay

The most convenient town to base yourself to begin exploring Faugères is Béziers. It's somewhat grey and run-down but it has its attractions. There's a broad, leafy promenade named after the town's most famous son, Paul Riquet, architect of the Canal du Midi which passes through the town. There's the old town beside the river Orb which is dominated by the imposing cathedral of St-Nazaire. And there are a couple of good museums (*see below*).

The best deluxe place to stay is the inexpensive, three-star Hôtel Imperator. Alternatively, there's the Hôtel des Poètes with rooms overlooking the Plateau des Poètes, a romantic garden with swans and ponds designed by the creators of the Bois de Boulogne in Paris. There are a few good places to dine in Béziers. The best is the elegant L'Ambassade while the inventive Le Framboisier is popular with locals.

Other things to do

In Béziers, the Hôtel Fabregat and the nearby Hôtel Fayet house collections of fine arts (tel: 04 67 28 38 78, and 04 67 49 04 66). The Musée de Biterrois (tel: 04 67 36 71 01) has an admirable collection of Gallo-Roman relics and ho-hum sections on natural history and ethnography. Béziers is a good place to embark on a cruise of the Canal du Midi into Minervois country (or just take a boat ride). You shouldn't miss the remarkable series of seven canal-locks in Béziers, Les Écluses de Fontséranes, and the Pont-Canal carrying the Canal du Midi over the river Orb. For more information on boat rental and tours contact Béziers Croisières (3 rue René Réaumur, 34500 Béziers, tel: 04 67 49 08 23).

GROWERS IN FAUGERES

Château des Estanilles
34480 Cabrerolles
Tel: 04 67 90 29 25 *(B4)*

Château de Grézan
34480 Laurens
Tel: 04 67 90 27 46 *(B3)*

Château la Liquière
34480 Cabrerolles
Tel: 04 67 90 29 20 *(B4)*

Domaine Alquier
34600 Faugères
Tel: 04 67 23 07 89 *(C3: moderate)*

Domaine La Croix Belle
34480 Puissalicon
Tel: 04 67 36 27 23 *(A2)*

Domaine du Météore
34480 Cabrerolles
Tel: 04 67 90 21 12 *(C4: inexpensive)*

Domaine St-Antonin
34480 Cabrerolles
Tel: 04 67 90 13 24 *(B4: moderate)*

PRICES: *expensive to moderate (other than where specified)*

St-Chinian

St-Chinian is the last terroir in the Hérault and better known in Anglophone countries than neighbouring Faugères to the east because it's bigger and its name is easier to say. Otherwise, St-Chinian has much in common with its neighbour to the east.

The monk Aniane

Like Faugères, St-Chinian was originally an appellation in its own right; it too became a *cru* of the Coteaux du Languedoc in 1985. The vineyards cover the rugged Cévennes foothills and are crossed by the rivers Orb and Vernazobre. There's more schist to the north and more limestone and clay to the south of the appellation.

The name St-Chinian comes from a ninth-century monk called Aniane who planted vines here and became St-Aniane (or Sanch Aniane, in Occitan). Viticulture has remained important in St-Chinian since the middle ages, largely because little else will grow here.

Travelling around

St-Chinian can be reached directly from Béziers along the N112, and a good first stop to find out more about St-Chinian's wines is the appellation's showcase on the main square in St-Chinian. The Maison des Vins carries wines from all the producers. St-Chinian itself is a small country town, but it's a hive of activity compared to sleepy Faugères.

For your wine travels, plan to spend a couple of days exploring the wine country and its attractions. If you are coming from Béziers, you can take either the D112 or the D154 out of Béziers and begin either west of St-Chinian in Assignan (*B4*), or in the east of the appellation at Murviel-lès-Béziers (*B1*).

If you begin in the east, visit Château Caujan in Murviel-lès-Béziers before setting off. Stop by at Château Cazal-Viel en route to picturesque Cessenon-sur-Orb; it's one of the few sizeable villages in the area, and is spread out around the vestiges of its ancient fortress beside the river Orb. It's fairly sleepy most of the time, but comes to life on market days, which are Tuesday and Saturday.

When you set off again, trun right off the D20 for Domaine des Jougla before continuing to St-Chinian. The village itself is ensconced in the Vernazobres Valley, west of Cessenon-sur-Orb. and is dominated by Mont Caroux and Mont Grange. Its eighteenth-century church is worth a detour. Head to the winery of Clos Bagatelle before leaving the village for Domaine Moulinier. Finally, your destination of Assignan offers the

BELOW *A peacock in a vineyard: they are said to be noisiest when rain is threatened, so should be relatively quiet round here.*

prospect of a visit to the go-ahead Domaine du Sacré-Coeur. To make the most of your time, a car is essential since public transport is very limited and a cycle would severely restrict the amount of ground you need to cover to visit the domaines featured here.

What the wines are like

St-Chinian wines typically come in two styles. The lighter wines come from the schistous slopes to the north of the appellation, with the more substantial wines coming from the limestone and clay slopes to the south. The cooperatives, like those of Berlou and Roquebrun, play leading roles.

Top growers in St-Chinian (*see* also p.136)

Domaine Moulinier
34360 Pierrerue,
tel: 04 67 38 03 97,
domaine-moulinier@wanadoo.fr
There's an impressive new *cave* amid the vines at this property outside St-Chinian. The young Pascal Moulinier is in charge of

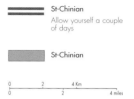

St-Chinian
Allow yourself a couple
of days

St-Chinian

0   2   4 Km
0   2   4 miles

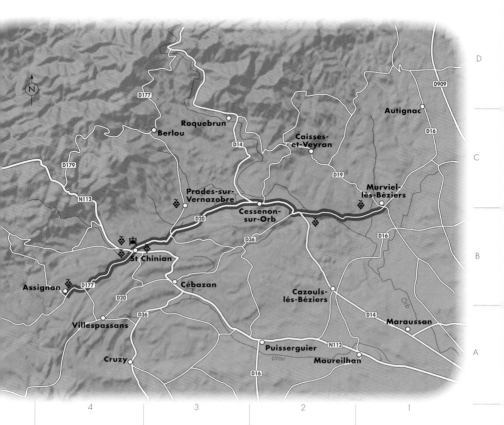

GROWERS IN ST-CHINIAN

Château Cazal-Viel
34460 Cessenon-sur-Orb
Tel: 04 67 89 63 15
The Miquels' château is in a beautiful part of the Orb Valley between Cessenon and Cazouls-lès-Béziers. Syrah dominates its stylish St-Chinians, like the elegant Cuvée des Fées and the flagship Les Larmes des Fées. *(B2: moderate to expensive)*

Château Caujan
34490 Murviel-lès-Béziers
Tel: 04 67 37 80 00
The Guy family has run this pioneering estate since 1868. Their non-Midi varietals and blends are commendable. Their AC white is full of southern fruit; their top AC reds are Gabrielle Spinola and Bois Joli. *Gîte* accommodation is available. *(C1: moderate)*

Clos Bagatelle
La Cave des 4 Vents
route de St-Pons
34360 St-Chinian
Tel: 04 67 93 61 63
This estate, at the end of an avenue of parasol pines, has been in the Simon family since 1623. Fans of Carignan should buy the Cuvée Camille, made from ninety-year-old vines. The top AC red is La Gloire de mon Père. *(B4: moderate)*

Domaine des Jougla
Prades-sur-Vernazobre
34360 St-Chinian
Tel: 04 67 38 06 02
The Jouglas' vines straddle two terroirs: one schist and the other clay. Their best St-Chinian red, the Cuvée Signée, comes from old vines planted on the former. *(B3: inexpensive)*

vinification. You might expect wines that are applauded, as these are, by the American critic Robert Parker to be overblown and oak-grained, but Pascal has a defter touch than that. Syrah is the grape of choice and there are three reds with increasing proportions of the variety in their blends.

The basic Tradition is great value, the mid-range Les Sigillaires undergoes a long maceration, and the top Les Terraces Grillées is a dense *vin de garde*. Also visit its Espace Vin boutique in St-Chinian for these and other French wines. *(B3: moderate to expensive)*

Domaine du Sacré-Coeur

ave de St-Chinian, 34360 Assignan, tel: 04 67 38 17 97
Locals viewed Marc Cabaret with suspicion when he came here from Bordeaux to make wine in 1991. Ten years later they made him president of the appellation. He clearly cares about St-Chinian and his wines are great-value examples of the AC. His everyday red has young Syrah, Grenache, and very old Carignan in equal measure.

The top red, Cuvée Kevin, with its refreshingly folksy name, is the same blend partly oaked. Both have mouthfuls of concentrated fruit and finesse. Cabaret also makes a superior Viognier *vin de pays* from very low yields and Muscat from vines in the Minervois. *(B4: inexpensive to moderate)*

Finding a place to stay

Accommodation options are limited in St-Chinian, however the attractive, modern Hôtel Le Pressoir is just 500m from the village's centre. Its sixteen spacious rooms are set around a swimming pool with mountain views. The restaurant serves a menu which includes a number of regional specialities.

Eating out should include a visit to Le Petit Nice in pretty Roquebrun, north of Cessenon-sur-Orb. Regional specialities from local ingredients are served on a terrace with panoramic views over the river Orb; afterwards you can wander around the Mediterranean garden nearby. Alternatively, there's the rustic La Calèche under an elegant stone arch on St-Chinian's esplanade, where Régis Pajani prepares traditional dishes with an original touch.

Other things to do

North of Béziers, the ruined twelfth-century Abbaye de Fontcaude outside Cazedarnes is tucked into a pretty valley and is worth a detour. It is about 10km (6 miles) east of St-Chinian, outside the village of Cazedarnes on the D134 and is also worth a detour (tel: 04 67 38 23 85; open every day from June 1 to September 30; Saturdays and Sunday afternoons the rest of the year, except January when it is open on Sunday afternoons only). It's hidden away in a pretty, isolated valley on the ancient pilgrimage route of St Jacques de -Compostelle. The name comes from a spring that runs at a constant temperature all year round, although it's not particularly hot, as the name suggests.

Not much remains of the original abbey, although the church's transept and apses are in very good condition. The renovated stained glass windows, reproduction furniture, and dazzling cloisters help to retain a medieval atmosphere of monastic life. There's a museum on site, too, containing fragments of masonry, columns and friezes.

During the summer, the abbey hosts concerts of both sacred and popular music.

Gothic treasures

About 10km (6 miles) south of the Abbaye de Fontcaude is the attractive canal village of Capestang on the Canal du Midi. It's worth a visit for its tall, unfinished gothic Collégiale St-Etienne – a sight which is visible for miles around. Nearby Quarante is also worth a detour. It's set in some of the loveliest countryside in the Languedoc, and boasts a remarkable and austere Romanesque church, the Abbataile Ste-Marie, which was built between the years 982 and 1053.

And, if you're planning where to stop for lunch, the park in the grounds of Château Rouière in Quarante is an idyllic spot for a picnic.

LEFT *A typical modern cellar, with both steel and new oak.*

BELOW *The Abbaye de Fontcaude, on the pilgrim route and boasting a hot spring.*

Southern Languedoc

Minervois and St-Jean-de-Minervois

The Minervois is the second largest appellation in the Aude after Corbières, and the two appellations are often regarded as twins. The vineyards cover a vast amphitheatre north of the Canal du Midi, between medieval Carcassonne and Roman Narbonne. To the north is the Montagne Noire and to the south the Corbières Massif. The landscape is like the Corbières, with patches of vines and olives covering wild, arid, rocky, and sparsely-populated hills. Neolithic dolmens and caves are scattered across the Montagne Noire foothills. By the Canal du Midi, large vineyards surround pretty villages. You can glide through Minervois wine country by canal-boat and bike. A narrow-gauge railway run by enthusiasts also crosses the region.

RIGHT *A shrine in the vineyards of Château de Gourgazaud.*

BELOW *The town and gorge of Minerve, first a Cathar centre and now a tourist destination.*

Wines of wisdom

Minervois takes its name from the isolated medieval village of Minerve in the northeast of the appellation, which in turn takes its name from the Roman goddess of wisdom, Minerva. The Romans were the first to cultivate vines here, mainly on the plain. The upper Minervois was cultivated later with the establishment of the monasteries. Minervois suffered more than most in the crusades against the Cathars, which included the siege of Minerve. By the eighteenth century, with the opening of the Canal du Midi, the area's fortunes picked up again, and wine has been increasingly important ever since.

In 1985, Minervois wines in all three colours gained AC status. In 1998, one terroir was singled out for *cru* status: La Livinière. It's a limestone and clay zone between Caunes-Minervois and La Livinière in the foothills of the Montagne Noire. Now producers are campaigning for other zones to be recognized for their special merits. From east to west, they are: Le Causse, around Minerve; Les Mourels, south of Minerve; Les Serres, in the southeast; Les Balcons de l'Aude, east of Carcassonne; and La Clamoux, in the

far west. Climate and soil differentiate these five zones, and producers argue that the wines are distinctive too.

What the wines are like

The Minervois typicity partly comes from the terroir. The vines cover a series of pebbly limestone, sandstone, and schist terraces that descend the Montagne Noire. These were formed by the rivers La Clamoux, L'Argent Double, L'Ognon, and La Cesse which run down the northern slopes of the Aude Valley. The weather is predominantly Mediterranean with some ocean influences to the west around La Clamoux, and some harsh winters around Le Causse to the north, which is 200m (660 feet) in altitude. The blend of grape varieties is typically Mediterranean – Carignan, Cinsault, Grenache, Syrah, and Mourvèdre. Young Minervois reds can have aromas of spicy blackcurrant and violets. Aged examples take on notes of candied fruit, prunes and even leather. Some of the whites undergo cask-ageing and the rosés tend to be made from Syrah.

The sweet, fortified Muscats from St-Jean-de-Minervois are made from the superior Muscat à Petits Grains. There are a variety of styles, but the trick is getting the balance right between alcohol and sugar. There's also an emphasis on freshness. The terroir here is a lunar-like limestone plateau.

How to get to the vineyards

You can visit by boat those Minervois domaines that are beside the Canal du Midi. Anything from a cruiser to a canoe and a bike can be hired at one of the pretty canal-side villages

LOCAL INFORMATION

Office de Tourisme
2 rue des Martyrs
34210 Minerve
Tel: 04 68 91 81 43

Syndicat d'Initiative
3 place de la Mairie
34210 Olonzac
Tel: 04 68 91 21 08

BOAT RENTAL:
Minervois Cruisers
38 chemin des Patiasses
Le Somail
11120 Ginestas
Tel: 04 68 46 28 52
boatyard@minervoiscruisers
.com
www.minervoiscruisers.com

TOURIST TRAIN: Autorail
Touristique de Minervois
53 ave Wilson
11200 Lézignan-Corbières
Tel: 04 68 27 05 94
www.atm.fr.tc
Sundays and holidays from July to September.

ABOVE *Best to telephone ahead to be sure of a welcome.rather than a closed door.*

═══ East: St-Jean-de-Minervois and La Livinière

═══ West: the rich and varied region of Minervois

Plan at least two days for exploring this area

▬ Côtes de Provence

▬ Coteaux Varois

between Béziers and Carcassonne, like Le Somail (A5). The Minervois is just 35km (22 miles) across but you'll cover a lot more ground than that visiting the domaines featured here. Public transport is not practical, cycling is an option but the best way is by car. Most of the domaines are well signposted. A good place for an overview of the appellation's wines and producers is Robert Eden's stylish tasting and sales outlet, La Tuilerie, housed in a converted tile factory just south of La Livinière. He's one of the area's most dedicated *vignerons* and he's also biodynamic. Try his Michelin-starred restaurant, Le Relais de Pigasse, by the Canal du Midi near La Croisade between Capestang and Argeliers.

Travelling around

There are a number of ways to criss-cross the Minervois as domaines are scattered between the Canal du Midi in the south and the foothills of the Montagne Noire in the north. Two routes are plotted here. The eastern route begins in the Muscat capital of St-Jean-de-Minervois in the extreme north of the appellation. Apart from sweet wines, including the historic Domaine de Barroubio, there's not much to detain you in this tiny commune of four hamlets. The route then passes through some beautiful, if sparsely populated, landscapes, past Oupia, where you should

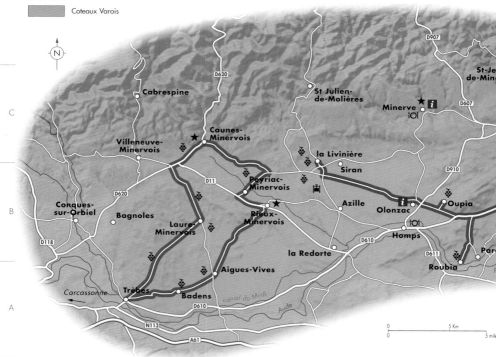

seek out the château of the same name, before arriving in Olonzac, the region's economic capital. The vestiges of the village's ancient ramparts are worth a look, but the real attraction is nearby: the river Ognon Pont-Canal, where the Canal du Midi traverses the river. This route ends in La Livinière, the capital of the best Minervois wines, and home to the châteaux of Gourgazaud and Ste-Eulalie and the marvellous Domaine Piccinini (*see below*).

For the western route, begin in nearby Rieux-Minervois. The village boasts a massive and austere château, a beautiful old stone bridge, and one of the uncanniest medieval churches in France – a seven-sided monument full of allegorical references to medieval mysticism. The route travels via Peyriac-Minervois, where the grandeur of the Hôtel Château de Violet beckons, past Caunes-Minervois, home of Domaine Villerambert-Julien, and also takes in Trèbes beside the Canal du Midi – the triple lock and the nearby Pont de la Rode are worth a detour – and the architecturally rich Caunes (it owes its wealth to the nearby marble quarries, which are a remarkable sight). Plan to spend at least two days exploring the area.

Top growers in Minervois (*see also p.136*)
Château Belvize
La Lecugne, 11120 Bize-Minervois, tel: 04 68 46 22 70
Château Belvize is set in picturesque and isolated countryside surrounded by vines, pines, cypress trees, and *garrigue* outside the village of Bize. It's on the eastern edge in the Les Mourels zone. The energetic and committed Fernando Truyols and Jean-Marie Desrues run the place. Their vineyards are a mosaic of varieties from which they make a range of excellent Minervois and *vins de pays*. Their Cuvée des Oliviers shows what a top Minervois red with ageing potential can be like. The Réserve and Tradition round off their range. If you're lucky, they might have some rare, sweet Minervois Noble too. (*C5: moderate*)

Château Pique-Perlou
12 ave des Ecoles, 11200 Roubia, tel: 04 68 43 22 46
An energetic young couple run this estate overlooking the Canal du Midi. The name means "to work in the hills" and their vineyards cover slopes around Pouzols in the Les Serres terroir. Their isolated vines include some very old Grenache and 100-year-old Carignan. Serge and Véronique Serris give their low-yielding grapes a long maceration and use younger Syrah and Mourvèdre in their

Minervois. The premium red is usually from late-harvested and overripe grapes fermented in wood. It's got great concentration and complexity. Look for their sweet Grenache Blanc from grapes with noble rot, and the crisp, dry white from the same grape. (*B5: moderate*)

Domaine de Barroubio
34360 St-Jean-de-Minervois, tel: 04 67 38 14 06, baroubio@club-internet.fr
The Miquels have been in this hamlet outside St-Jean-de-Minervois for five centuries. They make five or six fabulous sweet Muscats from grapes planted in very stony, hard, limestone soil. Both the wines and the Miquels are meticulous and highly regarded. Try the late-harvested *cuvées* and buy their lemony, honey-sweet classic Muscat. They also make superb Minervois reds and rosés. But, their Muscats are quite possibly the best in the Midi. (*C5: moderate to expensive*)

Domaine Piccinini
route des Meulières, 34210 La Livinière, tel: 04 68 91 44 32, fax: 04 68 91 58 65, domaine-piccinini@wanadoo.fr, www.domaine-piccinini.com
This is another good domaine producing incredibly good-value wines. Unfortunately, most are exported. Jean-Christophe Piccinini, a former oenology student whose father directed the La Livinière co-op, runs the estate. Two great *vins de pays*, a Chardonnay and a Merlot, but the best wines are the appellation whites, rosés, and reds. The white contains six or seven Midi varieties and it's richly aromatic and full of flavour. The rosé is pure Syrah. The Clos d'Angély red is from old vines, the Line et Laëtitia from older ones. They're both oaked and bursting with flavours of black fruits and the garrigue. A village *gîte* is now available. (*C3: moderate*)

Hôtel Château de Violet
route de Pépieux, 11160 Peyriac-Minervois, tel: 04 68 78 10 42 (hotel), 04 68 78 11 44 (cellar), chateau.de.violet@wanadoo.fr, www.chateau-de-violet.com
This grand, ornate château dates back to the eleventh century. It was remodelled in the seventeenth and nineteenth centuries and houses a characterful three-star hotel, restaurant, the winery and a viticulture museum, all set in lovely parkland. The whole is charming and authentic. The wines are classy too. Buy the pure Marsanne Minervois La Dame Blanche; it's one of the best whites around. Find space in your cellar for the Vieilles Vignes

ABOVE *A cobbled street in Minerve; not a town for high heels.*

RIGHT *Vineyards in the foothills of the Montagne Noire, which dominates the Minervois to the north.*

too, it's the top red with mouthfuls of oak-aged Mourvèdre. Cuvée Clovis is based on Syrah. They're great value. The busy website tells you where you can park your helicopter. (*B3: moderate*)

Finding a place to stay
Try the splendid three-star Hôtel Château de Violet in Peyriac. Alternatively, the Auberge de l'Arbousier in Homps is a charming old *mas* on the banks of the canal with one of the best restaurants in the Minervois. In Minerve, there's Le Relais Chantovent with seven rooms and a fine restaurant with a terrace overlooking the gorges (closed mid-November to March). Olonzac is the area's principal town and it's a good base too. Try the Hôtel du Park.

Other things to do
From July to September, enthusiasts run the ATM Minervois tourist train from Bize-Minervois to Narbonne. It takes in a number of attractions along the way. There's the Oulibo olive oil factory at Cabezac and excellent wines at Château Cabezac. At Sallèles d'Aude on the Canal du Midi, there's the Amphoralis pottery museum and excavation site. Le Somail has a quirky hat museum with 6,000 examples amassed by a private collector (Musée des Chapeaux, tel: 04 68 46 19 26). Minerve's museums are nothing to get excited about but just west of the village is the impressive pink Canyon de la Cesse. In Rieux-Minervois, you should stop to admire the mysterious seven-sided medieval church of Ste-Marie with its mystical and allegorical architecture. Roussillon's "Master of Cabestany" sculpted the interior and portals. Caunes-Minervois is an attractive town famous for its marble and its rambling Abbaye, founded in 780, with a sixteenth-century abbot's mansion.

WHERE TO STAY AND EAT

Auberge de l'Arbousier
50 ave de Carcassonne
11200 Homps
Tel: 04 68 91 11 24

Hôtel du Parc
18 ave de Homps
34210 Olonzac
Tel: 04 68 91 14 55

Le Relais Chantovent
17 Grand Rue
34210 Minerve
Tel: 04 68 91 14 18

Le Relais de Pigasse
RD5, 11590 Ouveillan
Tel: 04 58 89 40 98

La Tuilerie
34210 La Livinière
Tel: 04 58 91 42 63

Malepère and Cabardès

Nouth and south of Carcassonne and west of the Minervois and Limoux are the Languedoc's most westerly and overlooked vineyards: Cabardès and Malepère. They're the youngest appellations in the Languedoc and still working out their identity. Cabardès is summarized in the slogan "Vent d'Est, Vent d'Ouest", expressing the opposing climatic influences. It's a hilly region on the slopes of the Montagne Noire with pretty villages, including the renowned book-selling town of Montolieu. Lovers of pork and beans will relish a visit to Castelnaudary in the far west, home of *cassoulet*. Malepère is famous for the numerous circular villages scattered nearby.

BELOW *The village of Montréal, worth a visit for its gothic church.*

Travelling around

Cabardès' *vignerons* tend to occupy the sunny, south-facing slopes of the Montagne Noire, with the most important domaines being around Aragon, Montolieu, Conques-sur-Orbiel, and Mas-Cabardès. Six rivers flow across the natural amphitheatre of slopes, and vineyards are found between 100 and 350m (330 and 1,150 feet) in altitude. The river Orbiel separates Cabardès from Minervois country to the east and the Canal du Midi separates it from Malepère to the south.

Malepère *vignerons* are concentrated on the northern and southern slopes of the cone-shaped Malepère Massif at around 250m (820 feet) in altitude, with fewer producers on the smaller eastern and western slopes. The Massif itself reaches a peak of 442m (1,450 feet) at Mont Naut where animals graze but vines are not cultivated. It then slopes off to the Canal du Midi to the north, Castelnaudary to the west, the river Aude to the east and the Limoux vineyards to the south.

The Cabardès wine route is a circuit that, when travelled anti-clockwise, passes through the villages of Ventenac, lively little Pennautier, Villemoustaussou, Conques-sur-Orbiel, Villegailhenc, and Aragon. Ventenac is home to the château of the same name, Château Ventaiolle, and look out for Château de Brau when you near Villemoustoussou. At Conques-sur-Orbiel, allow time for a visit to Château de Salitis. Lastours, with its four châteaux, and Montolieu, with its numerous bookshops, are also worth a detour.

The Malepère wine route runs from Villesiscle (C4) in an arc south to Roullens (B2), joining the D623 and leaving at Cambieure. Before that turn, however, visit the historic Château de Routier, and when you rejoin in Malviès, visit Château Malviès-Guilhem (*see* p.111).

The main tourist attraction on the Cabardès-Malepère circuit is Carcassonne – the second most visited site in France (after Mont-St-Michel). It's on the edge of both appellations. Medieval Carcassonne, La Cité, is a must-see. It's a UNESCO World Heritage Site, fancifully renovated in the second half of the nineteenth century by the energetic Viollet-le-Duc, who also spruced up Narbonne.

The main attractions on the Malepère route include the circular village of Bram and tranquil little Montréal; its gothic church of St-Vincent boasts one of the most beautiful organs in France. Plan to spend at least three days exploring Cabardès, Malepère and Carcassonne.

Roman wine

Cabardès prospered in antiquity from forestry and iron- and gold-mining on the slopes of the Montagne Noire. The Romans

LOCAL INFORMATION

Office de Tourisme
15 blvd Camille Pelletan
11890 Carcassonne
Tel: 04 68 10 24 30
accueil@carcassonne-tourisme.com
www.carcassonne-tourisme.com

Cabardès
Beautiful countryside and friendly *vignerons*

Malepère
Tour the Massif where viticulture dominates the scene

Cabardès

Malepère

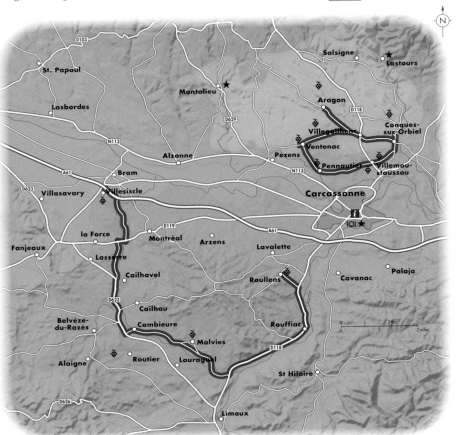

ABOVE *Viollet-le-Duc's restored medieval Carcassone.*

RIGHT *A range of agriculture exists in the south.*

WHERE TO STAY AND EAT

Hôtel Le Donjon
2 rue de Comte-Roger
11890 Carcassonne
Tel: 04 68 11 23 00

Hôtel du Pont Vieux
32 rue Trivalle
11890 Carcassonne
Tel: 04 68 25 24 99

Le Tirou
90 ave Monseigneur de Langle
11400 Castelnaudary
Tel: 04 68 94 15 95

cultivated olives and vines here, crops that became increasingly important with the expansion of the monasteries in the middle ages. In the thirteenth century, there was a boom in textiles, tanning, and mining.

The name Cabardès comes from the local Barons of Cabaret who defended Château de Lastours during the gruesome campaigns against the Cathars in that century. A period of economic decline set in afterwards. However, the wines of Cabardès received some praise in the eighteenth century, before phylloxera put an end to the area's viticultural fortunes for nearly a hundred years. In the 1960s, *vignerons* began planting Bordeaux varieties. Since 1999, red and rosé Cabardès have enjoyed AC status.

The name Malepère means "bad rock", which bodes well for vines, and indeed viticulture dominates the landscape. South of Cabardès, Malepère marks the Languedoc's western frontier. Viticulture here goes back to the Roman occupation too but it wasn't until the eleventh century, following a succession of invasions, that winemaking took off: with the opening of the Canal du Midi, the wines found a wider market. The area suffered after the arrival of phylloxera and, like Cabardès, took time to recover. The area's suitability for Bordeaux varieties was noticed in the 1960s and the fortunes of the appellation picked up. As in Cabardès, there are no AC white wines in Malepère.

What the wines are like

The style of both appellations comes from a mixture of Bordeaux and Mediterranean grapes, although the former play a bigger role in westerly Malepère. Cabardès tends to be drier, windier, and warmer and includes more Mediterranean varieties, especially Syrah but not Carignan. Only a bold sommelier, however, would wager a bet on distinguishing one from the other in a blind tasting.

There tend to be two styles of red, the first for drinking young and the other for ageing in bottle. The latter are yet to be found in great number. Generally, the young reds have juicy red- and black-fruit flavours. Cooperatives dominate production in Malepère, whereas there are more independents in Cabardès.

Finding a place to stay

Carcassonne is a great place to base yourself and there's no shortage of good accommodation, though staying in the old *cité* can be expensive and noisy in the summer. The surprisingly affordable three-star Hôtel le Donjon is three medieval houses turned into one, with a shaded garden and gourmet restaurant. A better bet, with views of the *cité*, is to stay in the *ville basse* (the medieval "low town"). Just outside the old city walls is the quaint two-star Hôtel du Pont Vieux. If you make it to Castelnaudary, you'll have reached what the French call *le partage des eaux* ("the watershed") where the Atlantic southwest meets the Midi. If you want to eat *cassoulet* then the best place, Le Tirou on the east side of town, is near the eighteenth-century apothecary, l'Apothicairerie.

Other things to do

Montolieu (*D3*) re-invented itself during the 1990s as a book town. It hosts an annual summer book fair, there's a museum of bookbinding and printing, and there are a number of secondhand bookshops. Nearby Lastours hosts a sound-and-light spectacle at the former Cathar stronghold on Thursday and Sunday evenings during July and August (tel: 04 68 77 16 76).

Top growers in Malèpere and Cabardès (*see also* p.137)

Château Malviès-Guilhem

11300 Malviès, tel: 04 68 31 14 41,
www.chateauguilhem.com

This handsome eighteenth-century château set southwest of Carcassonne was built on the ruins of a Roman villa. Brigitte and Bernard Gourdou-Guilhem still find the odd Roman fragment in the vineyards. Their fruity Malepère Tradition deserves to be enjoyed young and slightly chilled. There's an unusual sweet, late-picked Sauvignon, Marquis d'Auberjon. It's the priciest wine in a good-value range. (*B3: inexpensive*)

Domaine de Cabrol

D118, 11600 Aragon, tel: 04 68 77 19 06

Vines have been cultivated here since the sixteenth century. The south-facing vineyards cover slopes at some 250m (820 feet), overlooking Carcassonne. Brothers Claude and Michel Carayol produce two reds that show the Cabardès personality – named after the appellation's slogan. Their Cuvée Vent d'Est is mostly Syrah with Grenache and Cabernet, while the Cuvée Vent d'Ouest is mostly Cabernet with Grenache and Syrah. To put it crudely, the former is supple whereas the latter is firm. They're both top Cabardès wines. (*D2: inexpensive to moderate*)

GROWERS IN MALEPERE AND CABARDES

Château de Brau

11620 Villemoustoussou
Tel: 04 68 72 31 92
This is the place to find well-made, organic Cabardès and *vins de pays*. Buy the red Cuvée Exquise and drink it in five years or the Tradition to enjoy now. (*C1: inexpensive*)

Château de Salitis

11600 Conques-sur-Orbiel
Tel: 04 68 77 16 10
Anne Marandon makes satisfying wines at this former outpost of Lagrasse Abbey in the Corbières.Try her Cabardès Cuvée Premium. (*D1: inexpensive*)

Château Ventaillole

11610 Ventenac
Tel: 04 68 24 92 74
This historic estate stresses the Midi side of the Cabardès personality, tucked away amid pines and *garrigue* on south-facing slopes outside Ventenac. (*D2: inexpensive*)

Château de Ventenac

11610 Ventenac
Tel: 04 68 24 93 42
Alain Maurel has created a leading Cabardès estate. Buy traditional Cabardès, which is great value for money. For an oak-aged experience, try Cuvée les Pujols. (*D2: inexpensive*)

Limoux and the Upper Aude Valley

Blanquette de Limoux is said, especially by the locals, to be the world's oldest sparkling wine. The method of fermenting the wine in bottle for a second time is said to have been invented here, and you can visit the Benedictine abbey of St-Hilaire east of Limoux where it all began. Limoux is a bustling town in the Aude Valley south of Carcassonne and the Massif of Malepère and north of the Pyrénées. It's a wild, hilly and sheltered region that's cooler than the neighbouring Corbières to the east and Roussillon to the south, making it perfect for white wines. The wine is great value for money, and far more affordable than Champagne for drinking every day.

An earlier sparkle
Legend says that in 1531 a monk at St-Hilaire noticed that the wine he'd left in the autumn gave off bubbles in the spring. He figured out why, controlled the process and the rest is history. What happened? Well, the cold winter stopped the wine from fermenting completely. When warmer temperatures arrived in the spring, the wine began to ferment again. And when the monk tasted it, the wine fizzed with the carbon dioxide from the second fermentation. *Et viola*, Blanquette de Limoux was born. He must have been a hit with his brothers.

Before this breakthrough, Limoux already had a reputation for its fine, still wines. The Romans praised them and accounts from the Middle Ages confirm that Limoux's winemakers hadn't lost their touch by then. The most recent addition to the appellation, the still Limoux Blanc, may actually be the oldest style. All the same, Blanquette de Limoux and Méthode Ancestrale were the first to gain appellation status. They earned their stripes in 1938, shortly after the creation of the AC system, and so became the Aude's first ACs. Crémant de Limoux was added in 1990 and three years later Limoux Blanc was elevated. Only a couple of dozen *vignerons* out of about 540 produce their own wine and one big cooperative dominates the appellation. Fortunately, it produces very good Limoux.

How to get to the vineyards
The domaines to visit are in a radius of around 20km (12 miles) around Limoux. The best way to visit them is by car, since cycling involves some steep climbs. Except for the lovely scenery, there's not much to distract you from wine tasting either, although you'll want to visit the famous abbeys of St-Hilaire and St-Polycarpe while you're near those villages.

BELOW *Shady streets and brightly painted shops make towns in the South a delight to explore.*

Travelling around

The Limoux wine route begins in Cépie, in the north, and follows the river Aude south to Limoux before heading for the hills and the wine villages of Tourreilles, Roquetaillade, Conilhac, and Antugnac. The route rejoins the upper Aude Valley around Moutazels and ends in the south of the appellation at Couiza, where the sixteenth-century Château des Ducs de Joyeuse is a must-see. The main attraction on the D118 between Limoux and Couiza is the medieval spa town of Alet-les-Bains, which boasts a mineral-water swimming pool that's unique in Europe, and some beautifully preserved architecture. You'll want to spend time discovering Limoux and exploring the mysteries of Rennes-le-Château (*see* below). Plan to spend a couple of days in the area to visit the domaines and see the sights.

What the wines are like

There are four of them: Blanquette de Limoux, Méthode Ancestrale, Crémant de Limoux, and Limoux Blanc. The first contains mostly Mauzac with a little

LOCAL INFORMATION

Office de Tourisme
promenade du Tivoli
11300 Limoux
Tel: 04 68 31 11 82
limoux@fnotsi.net

━━━ Limoux
Allow a couple of days to
make the most of this area

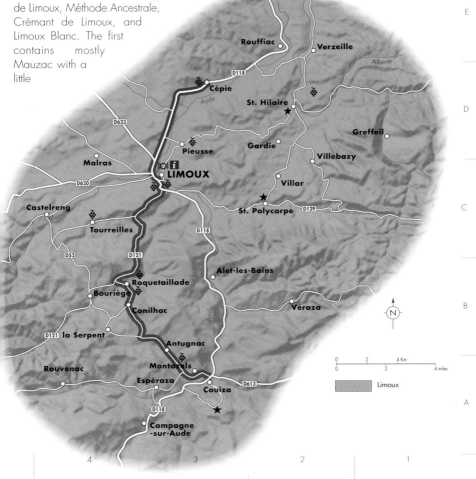

ABOVE *Limoux's Abbaye St-Hilaire, the* fons et origen *of fizz, according to the locals.*

RIGHT *An alternative way to tour.*

Chardonnay and Chenin Blanc. It can be *brut, sec, demi-sec* or *doux* depending on the sweetening *dosage* added after the second fermentation. Méthode Ancestrale is pure Mauzac. It's naturally sweet and light in alcohol as its fermentation proceeds without the second addition of yeast and sugar, unlike Blanquette. Crémant has more Chardonnay than Blanquette, making it richer on the palate. It's fermented like Blanquette but spends longer ageing in the barrel on its lees.

The still Limoux Blanc is a blend of all three grapes (usually with just a drop of Mauzac and a big helping of Chardonnay). It's vinified and aged in oak and released after the May following the vintage. Having said all that, the best producers ignore the regulations when they feel they're too restrictive. They often include more Chardonnay than the rules permit and sometimes add Pinot Noir, although that's not allowed – but it can make better wine.

Moves are underway to define Limoux's terroir with greater precision. Four sub-zones have been identified: Autan, centred on Limoux in the north, Haut-Vallée in the south, Méditerranéen to the east, and cooler Océanique to the west. The zones vary in temperature, humidity, altitude, geology, and aspect.

Top growers in Limoux and the Upper Aude (*see* also p.138)

Château Rives-Blanques
11300 Cépie, tel: 04 68 31 43 20, www.rives-blanques.com
One of the oldest domaines in the Limoux appellation is Rives-Blanques on the cusp of the Méditerranéen and Océanique terroirs. Since 2001, the environmentally friendly Jan and Caryl Panman have owned the place. Its vineyards are high on a plateau at 350m (1,148 feet) with lots of *galets* (large round, flat stones also found in parts of Châteauneuf-du-Pape). It makes three lovely Limoux Blancs. Cuvée de l'Odyssée is barrel-fermented and oak-aged Chardonnay with a drop of Mauzac, worthy of

ageing. Cuvée Occitania is pure Mauzac, and Dédicace is mostly Chenin Blanc. A good Blanquette has floral and honey notes that will develop over time. Enjoy the views over the Pyrénées to the south as you sip. (*D3: inexpensive to moderate*)

Domaine de Fourn
11300 Pieusse, tel: 04 68 31 15 03
A winding road leads up to the tiny village of Pieusse in the hills above the river Aude just north of Limoux. The largest domaine in the appellation, de Fourn produces a range of impressive wines. Grapes have been hand-picked since the family began producing wine here in 1937. Its Dame Robert is arguably the best *crémant* in the appellation. Ane, its good (still) Limoux is a subtly oaked Chardonnay. There's also a rich, honeyed Ancestrale. (*D3: inexpensive to moderate*)

Finding a place to stay
Accommodation in Limoux is limited. The Grand Hôtel Moderne et Pigeon is a luxury, three-star hotel with the best restaurant in town. Alternatively, the two-star Hôtel des Arcades has seven rooms and a restaurant. If you feel like staying amid vines, Domaine Martinolles has a *gîte* for five. Limoux is a pleasant town and a good place to base yourself and is liveliest during the carnivals from January to March. The arcaded place de la République is a broad, picturesque square in the centre of town with cafés and restaurants, and streets itching to be explored radiating from it. Nearby, in place du Presbytère is the gothic St-Martin church with fine stained glass. The charming Musée Petiet has a fine collection of Belle Époque, Impressionist and Pointillist paintings (tel: 04 68 31 85 03).

Other things to do
Fans of a good mystery will love Rennes-le-Château, perched in the Haut-Vallée south of Couiza. It was here that parish priest Bérganger Saunière lived a life of uncommon luxury, building himself a splendid villa where he entertained the personalities of the day. He died in 1917 and his church is said to include secret symbols that point to the source of his wealth. It's thought he discovered the lost treasure of the Cathars in a pillar beneath the old altar while he was renovating the church. It's possible too that he siphoned off some of the Comtesse de Paris' donation that funded the works, but his sudden and substantial wealth coincided with something he found in the church. There's more on him in the village museum and you can visit his estate.

GROWERS IN LIMOUX AND THE UPPER AUDE VALLEY

Les Caves du Sieur d'Arques
11300 Limoux
Tel: 04 68 74 63 00
This ambitious co-op has 750 members and makes three-quarters of all Limoux wines. Visit its vast underground cellars and see if terroir makes a difference, since there are Chardonnays from each of Limoux's four zones. (*C3: moderate*)

Domaine Collin
11300 Tourreilles
Tel: 04 68 31 35 49
This estate belongs to a Champagne man and his Perpignan wife. Their fabulous Cuvée Prestige shows what Chardonnay and Pinot Noir (unofficially) can do for Blanquette. (*C4: moderate*)

Domaine de Flassian
11300 Limoux
Tel: 04 68 31 15 88
The Antechs are growers but they also buy grapes from small producers with whom they work closely. Their best Blanquette is the Chardonnay-rich Cuvée d'Exception. (*C3: inexpensive to moderate*)

Corbières

W est of historic Narbonne and south of the Canal du Midi is the wild, vast, and hilly Corbières, the largest appellation in the Aude. Montagne d'Alaric and Mont Tauch dominate the landscape. This is Cathar country where magnificent ruined hilltop castles like Quéribus and Peyrepertuse dot the landscape. The abbeys of Fontefroide and Lagrasse are also on the wine route. Embedded within Corbières are the two Fitou zones, one by the sea and one inland around Mont Tauch. East of Narbonne on a spectacular promontory is the top Coteaux du Languedoc *cru* of La Clape. The Massif was an island in the Middle Ages before the Aude silted up, and its valleys contain the driest and most sun-soaked vineyards in the region.

An old wine

Corbières has endured a long and turbulent history. Under the Roman emperor Augustus the vineyards enjoyed considerable expansion. Overproduction has been a problem ever since, culminating in Corbières' contribution to the European wine lake of the late twentieth century. The earliest viticultural crisis dates back to 91 AD when the emperor Domitian ordered half the vines to be uprooted, following condemnation of the wines from Narbonne by transalpine producers.

Viticulture took off again between the eleventh and thirteenth centuries under the aegis of the Cistercians and Benedictines. However, the campaigns against the Cathars brought desolation to the vineyards. By the eighteenth century the vineyards were re-established and Corbières wine was being celebrated as far away as Russia. Then phylloxera struck in the nineteenth century and vineyards were replanted with high-yielding varieties. Overproduction returned and prompted a crisis at the beginning of the twentieth century. To promote quality over quantity, Corbières producers were encouraged to have appellation ambitions. However, the fear of higher taxes dissuaded them from applying early for AC status. The appellation was finally granted to red, rosé, and white Corbières wines in 1985, the same year that La Clape became a Coteaux du Languedoc *cru*.

What the wines are like

Corbières is red wine country with just tiny amounts of rosé and white. Historically the reds were robust, alcoholic, and often blended with lighter wines. Nowadays they have more identity, though some inferior Corbières is still found on supermarket shelves. Carignan dominates with the usual Midi varieties making up the blend. The young reds are full of black fruit flavours; mature versions have spicy notes of the *garrigue*. Wines for cellaring are generally powerful and full-bodied and develop gamey aromas of old leather, coffee, and cocoa. Mourvèdre and Syrah make up a higher proportion of the La Clape blends. Around La Clape, look for Carthagène, the local sweet dessert or apéritif wine.

There's an enormous variety of microclimates across Corbières. The vineyards also vary tremendously in altitude and soil type. A total of eleven distinct terroirs have been identified, of which the best known are Boutenac and Durban. It's easy to see the two Fitou terroirs as Corbières variants too. However, the factor that most influences the wine here is the *vigneron*. There are many ambitious young talents in the area.

How to get to the vineyards

This is sparsely populated territory, hostile to public transport and a challenge for all but the fittest cyclists. The best advice is to take the car and enjoy the views. Heading west from Narbonne, a tour of Corbières should take in the capital,

ABOVE *The Canal du Midi defines the northern Corbières boundary.*

LEFT *Montagne de la Clape, centre of the eponymous cru.*

Lézignan, where there's a good wine museum. From there, vineyards stretch west towards Carcassonne but the heartland is south towards Boutenac and Durban. The La Clape vineyards are just east of Narbonne towards Narbonne-Plage.

Travelling around

The wine route around La Clape, east of Narbonne, follows the D168 towards Narbonne-Plage and then picks up the D332 south to Gruissan and around the western side of the Massif. A number of small, winding tracks take you into the Massif where a number of producers are located. The main attraction between Narbonne-Plage and Gruissan is the new Cité de la Vigne et du Vin, a splendid wine science museum. Heading west, out of Narbonne, takes you into Corbières country where charming Lézignan is a good place to start (*D2*). From there you can take the D212 south to Fabrezan, Lagrasse (where the abbey is a must-see), and Villerouge-Termenès. Then head east to tiny Albas and on to the former stronghold of Durban where the château and church of St-Just are worth checking out. The

Corbières
Picturesque wine villages and fine domaines await you

Corbières

Fitou

0   2 Km
0   2 miles

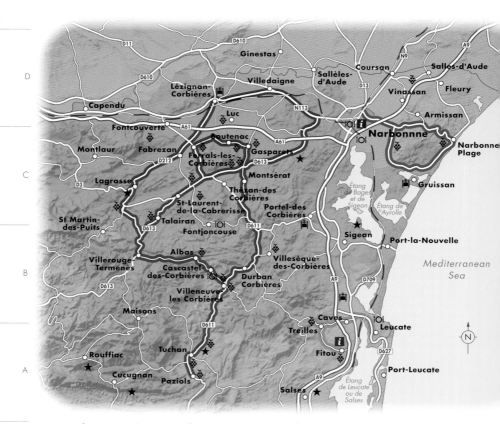

D611 takes you north through numerous wine villages to the Boutenac area where many fine domaines are located. Don't miss Fontefroide Abbey when heading back to Narbonne on the D613. Plan to spend at least three days discovering the Corbières and La Clape wine country, plus Narbonne.

Top growers in Corbières (see also p.138)

Château de Caraguilhes
11220 St-Laurent-de-la-Cabrerisse, tel: 04 68 27 88 99
This beautiful estate is set in 1,000ha of garrigue on a hillside 15km (9 miles) west of Fontefroide Abbey. The Montredon dynasty began building the château in the sixteenth century and owned it until 1908. For much of the last half of the twentieth century, the Faivre family owned it, converted it to organic viticulture and established its reputation. Burgundy négociant Laurent Max now owns it and continues the tradition. The three excellent whites and reds are, in ascending order of excellence, Classique, Prestige, and Solus. (C2: moderate to expensive)

Château Rouquette-sur-Mer
La Clape, 11100 Narbonne-Plage, tel: 04 68 49 90 41
Dating back to the fourteenth century, the original fortified château is now a pretty ruin amid pine trees and garrigue facing the sea. The Boscary family own the property and they're keen to enhance the place's natural beauty. To that end they planted 20,000 trees across their 400ha. The vineyards are south-facing on a series of terraces scattered amid aromatic garrigue. The wines come in three colours. They are, in order of excellence, the château wine, Clos de la Tour, and Henry Lapierre. There are two sparkling wines, a white and a rosé, and apéritifs. (C4: inexpensive to moderate)

Domaine Fontsainte
route Ferrals, 11200 Boutenac, tel: 04 68 27 07 63
Young Bruno Laboucarie increasingly takes the reins at this top family domaine in the Boutenac terroir. Viticulture here goes back at least five centuries, and Roman coins have been unearthed in the vineyards. The pride of the vineyard is some 100-year-old Carignan, the supple backbone of the reds. The rich La Demoiselle red is oak-aged, the excellent basic cuvée is not. The estate also makes a delicate, pale Gris de Gris rosé from five Midi varieties. It's one of the best in the Midi. Excellent value. Telephone ahead. (C2: moderate)

Domaine Haut-Gléon
Villesèque-des-Corbières, 11360 Durban, tel: 04 68 48 85 95, www.hautgleon.com
Pretty Haut-Gléon's history is ancient, baronial, and bloody. A

GROWERS IN CORBIERES

Château Ollieux Romanis
RD613, 11200 Montséret
Tel: 04 68 43 32 74
As the name suggests, viticulture here goes back to Gallo-Roman times. Look for the Roussanne-Marsanne white Prestige and the unusual pure Alicante red. The red Prestige keeps eight years or more. (C2: moderate)

Château Les Palais
11220 St-Laurent-de-la-Cabrerisse
Tel: 04 68 44 01 63
The origins of this picturesque estate between Lézignan and St-Laurent-de-la-Cabrerisse are religious rather than baronial. The chapel is an attractive tasting room. Buy the excellent red or white Randolin. (C2: inexpensive to moderate)

Domaine des Pensées Sauvages
11360 Albas, Tel: 04 68 45 81 30, www.le-guide.com/sauvagewine
"Hand-made and original" describe the characterful red wines of English couple Nick and Clare Bradford. In exceptional years they make a cuvée Réserve. Give it five years in the bottle if you can wait. (B2: moderate)

Domaine Serres-Mazard
Le Cellier St-Damien
11220 Talairan
Tel: 04 68 44 02 22
Buy the fruity château reds, the semi-sweet white L'Orchidée, and the aromatic dry Blanc de Blancs in the Mazard's friendly cave. in the heart of the old iron-mining town of Talairan. Two attractive gîtes. (C2: moderate)

ABOVE *The Abbaye de Fontefroide, one of the region's must-sees.*

RIGHT *The village of Fitou, one of nine villages to visit in the region.*

Gallo-Roman villa originally occupied the site north of Durban. In 1223, the Treilles family built a feudal castle here and took the title Marquis de Gléon. In 1830, the last Marquis and his son were murdered, and the surviving Marquise sold the estate in 1861. In 1991, the Duhamel family purchased the higher part of the estate, renovated the vineyard and cellars, and created six attractive *chambres d'hôtes*. Their stylish wines come in a distinctive, heavy bottle. The best red is named after the year's artist-in-residence. A leading domaine. (*B3: moderate to expensive*)

Finding a place to stay

Basing yourself in Narbonne is a sensible choice that allows you to return to civilization after a day in the wilderness. There's the quiet and comfortable three-star La Résidence, a converted nineteenth-century *hôtel particulière* (private mansion) near the cathedral and the Pont Voltaire. Or there's the grand and excellent-value La Dorade on the canal in the centre. Dining out in Narbonne offers plenty options, but the Michelin-starred La Table St-Crescent at the Palais des Vin should be on your agenda. It's Narbonne's best restaurant and it's in an eighteenth-century oratory set amid vineyards and olive groves with a vine-covered terrace. Or try the excellent Auberge du Vieux Puits in Fontjoncouse for its Mediterranean cuisine.

Other things to do

Visit the impressive subterranean cellars of Terra Vinea, the cellar and museum complex of Les Caves Rocbère, a group uniting three co-ops: Portel, Sigean, and Peyriac-de-Mer (tel: 04 68 48 64 90, www.terra-vinea.com).

WHERE TO STAY AND EAT

Auberge du Vieux Puits
5 ave de St-Victor
11360 Fontjoncouse
Tel: 04 68 44 07 37

La Dorade
44 rue Jean-Jaurès
11100 Narbonne
Tel: 04 68 32 65 95

La Résidence
6 rue du 1er Mai
11100 Narbonne
Tel: 04 68 31 19 41

La Table St-Crescent
Palais des Vins
route de Perpignan
11100 Narbonne
Tel: 04 68 41 37 37

Fitou

F itou is the Languedoc's oldest red wine appellation and the most southerly. Its Roman name was "Fita", meaning "frontier", as the town was the last trading post in Gaul before Iberian Catalonia. There are actually two Fitous embedded within the much larger Corbières appellation, straddling the ancient Via Domitia (today's A9 – *see* map, p.118). Haut-Fitou is rugged, hilly, wild-boar country dominated by Mont Tauch and medieval Château Aguilar. It's popular for outdoor activities, while Fitou Maritime's sandy beaches and lagoons attract holidaymakers and windsurfers. Despite its split personality, producers are unequivocal about what gives Fitou its typicity: Carignan.

Fitou times two

The Greeks planted the first vines in Fitou along the coastal zone and the Romans later developed these vineyards. However, Fitou's historical position as a border town ensured a turbulent past, including invasions by Barbarians, Visigoths, Moors, and anti-Cathar crusaders. As a result of centuries of upheavals, it wasn't until the seventeenth and eighteenth centuries that red Fitou wines gained widespread recognition. In 1948, they were given their appellation.

Differences in geology and climate distinguish the two Fitous. The Haut-Fitou zone is characterized by its shallow schist soils and pebbly terraces that cover a basin around the appellation's two principal villages, Tuchan and Paziols. Maritime influences are tempered here by the surrounding Corbières hills and conditions are hotter and drier than along the coast. The Fitou Maritime zone is predominantly clay and limestone with vineyards subject to influences from the sea and the lakes that dot the coastline. There are corresponding differences in grape varieties and wine styles, although these differences are slight.

How to get there

There are nine villages to visit across the two Fitou zones. In northern Haut-Fitou, at the southern end of the dramatic Berre gorge, there's the tiny former mining village of Cascatel and neighbouring Villeneuve-les-Corbières. To the south there's the market town of Tuchan and quaint Paziols with its Mexican-style chapel and friendly café. Fitou Maritime runs along low-lying hills and includes the

LOCAL INFORMATION

. . . .

Office de Tourisme
6 ave de la Mairie
11510 Fitou
Tel: 04 68 45 69 11

villages of Treilles, Caves, Fitou, Leucate, and Lapalme. The ancient, picturesque village of Treilles is perched on rocks around the ruins of a former château in the last of the Corbières back-country. The surrounding windfarms are a reminder that this is gusty countryside. An eleventh-century château overlooks old Fitou where traditional troglodyte houses with painted carved doors are hewn from the hillside. The former shepherd's hamlet of Caves is between Treilles and colourful, seaside Leucate with its white cliffs (*"leukas"* means "white" in Greek). The pretty market town of Lapalme is in the north of the zone.

Ambitious cyclists will enjoy discovering the two Fitous on two wheels. The spectacular D205 from Villeneuve to Embres and the D27 (the Feuilla Pass) between Embres and Treilles is especially popular for its slow, winding ascent. Less energetic types will want to take the car and drive the wine routes at a leisurely pace. There's quite a lot of ground to cover and, as usual, public transport is very much out of the question.

A good place to get an overview of the appellation is the impressive Maison des Vignerons de Fitou (RN9, 11510 Fitou, tel: 04 68 45 71 41) at the junction of the N9 and D709. It's a purpose-built facility with maps, models, aerial views, and archaeological documents. The nearby chapel of St-Pancrace was built on the site of a Roman villa. You'll want to allow yourselves a couple of days to explore this area.

BELOW *The rugged terrain of Corbières could still have many potentially excellent vineyard sites.*

Travelling around (*see* map, p.118)

Just 15km (9 miles) long, the Haut-Fitou wine route begins either in sleepy Paziols, in the south, or in even sleepier Cascatel-des-Corbières, in the north, home of the organic Domaine Grand Guilhem. The D611 conveniently links these villages and crosses the appellation's stunning landscapes. Having visited the many *vignerons* dotted around Tuchan, including Domaine de Rolland, Château Nouvelles, and the pioneering Mont Tauch co-op, head east to the magnificent fortified Château Aguilar (one of the five "sons of Carcassonne", along with Puilaurens, Quéribus, Peyrepertuse, and Termes). Energetic types will also want to hike up to La Récufa Vierge, east of Villeneuve-les-Corbières, for stunning views before stopping by the Domaine Lerys' winery.

For Fitou Maritime, take the D205 and D27 from Villeneuve, or the D39 and D9 from Tuchan, to pretty Treilles, touching down at Domaine Loubatière. Then head to seaside Leucate, via Caves, before heading for the appellation's capital, Fitou, stopping en route for the historic Château Abelanet. The Maritime route is around 10km (6 miles).

What the wines are like

Fitou wines are in fact not that much different from those of surrounding Corbières. Nevertheless, late-ripening Mourvèdre

is more common in the coastal Fitou wines, where it enjoys the Maritime climate, while the early-ripening Syrah is more common in Haut-Fitou. The other allowed grape varieties are Carignan and Grenache. Fitou reds have a reputation for keeping longer than their Corbières counterparts and they tend to be somewhat more robust and complex, with aromas of red fruits, pepper, prunes, and the *garrigue*. Aged in oak they are generally quite alcoholic and full-bodied – properties they share with wines from Roussillon to the south.

The co-ops dominate Fitou's production, with one in particular, the forward-looking Producteurs de Mont-Tauch, playing a particularly significant role. Based in Tuchan, it's the union of several smaller Fitou village

co-ops. The Maritime zone also has important co-ops in Leucate, Lapalme and Fitou itself. There are about thirty-five independent producers. Moves are underway to promote some Fitous as *grands crus*, and to establish a white Fitou AC.

Top growers in Fitou (*see* alsp p.139)
Château Abélanet
7 ave de la Mairie, 11510 Fitou,
tel: 04 68 45 76 50
Régis Abélanet traces his family's holdings back to 1697 (twelve generations). The family was instrumental in establishing the Fitou appellation. A leading producer, Abélanet has two styles of Fitou, the fruity, supple Tradition, and the rich, concentrated Vieilles Vignes. Also try the remarkable still and sparkling Maccabeu, and the rosé. The cellar is opposite the Mairie in Fitou and sells to a loyal clientele. (*A3: inexpensive to moderate*)

Château Nouvelles
11350 Tuchan, tel: 04 68 45 40 03,
www.chateaudenouvelles.com
The Daurat family's impressive estate is ensconced in its own magnificent valley 3km (2 miles) north of Tuchan where once a Roman villa and later a medieval castle stood. Château Aguilar overlooks the vineyards. Arriving in 1834, the Daurats began to establish a reputation for Fitou, bottling their first wines before World War II. In modern cellars, old *foudres* are used. Buy their excellent Fitou, especially the Vieilles Vignes, and try their range of sweet Rivesaltes. (*A2: moderate*)

Finding a place to stay
A number of domaines offer accommodation, like Domaine Lerys or Domaine Grand Guilhem. Alternatively, there's the modern and comfortable seaside Hôtel Méditerranée in Port-La-Nouvelle, north of Lapalme, whose restaurant specializes in seafood. In nearby Sigean there's the lovely Hôtel Le Ste-Anne. Its restaurant offers seasonal specialities. Eating out should include a visit to Jean-Marc Gautier's (*see* Domaine Gautier p.123) baroque-style seafood and grill restaurant La Closerie in Leucate with its grand piano set in an ancient wine cellar. In Villeneuve, try Le Corbièrou, where you can enjoy sea and mountain specialities in a warm, country-style ambiance.

Other things to do
North of Lapalme at Sigean there's Europe's largest African game reserve (Reserve Africaine de Sigean, tel: 04 68 48 20 20; www.reserveafricainesigean.fr). South of Fitou is a striking fifteenth-century Spanish fort at Salses (tel: 04 68 38 60 13).

WHERE TO STAY AND EAT
· ·

La Closerie
101 bis ave Jean Jaurès
11370 Leucate
Tel: 04 68 40 07 91

Le Corbièrou
21 ave Hautes-Corbières
11360 Villeneuve-les-Corbières
Tel: 04 68 45 83 05

Hôtel Méditerranée
blvd St-Charles
11210 Port-La-Nouvelle
Tel: 04 68 48 03 08

Hôtel Le Ste-Anne
3 ave Michel de L'Hospital
11130 Sigean
Tel: 04 68 48 24 38

Roussillon

Côtes du Roussillon and Rivesaltes

France's most southerly and sunny vineyards are in Roussillon. They follow the course of three rivers that begin in the Pyrénées, cross the Roussillon plain and end in the Mediterranean. Roussillon is a natural amphitheatre formed by Corbières to the north, Mont Canigou to the west, and the Albères foothills to the south. Many French sweet dessert and apéritif wines come from here, but producers are increasingly also making some of the most characterful red, rosé, and white wines in the Midi. This is Catalan country, but you don't need to speak the language to get by. The capital is vibrant Perpignan, one of France's most cosmopolitan cities. If you're here in July and August, there is a carnival every Thursday called *Jeudis à Perpignan*.

Twenty-five years of change

Extraordinary changes have taken place in Roussillon in the last twenty-five years. Vineyards have been restructured, cellars modernized, and young *vignerons* have been withdrawing from co-ops to make their own wine. Investment, optimism, hard work, and marketing are paying off. Winemakers are today developing reputations as far away as Japan, the USA, and Australia. Not long ago, however, the young were fleeing the family farm to pursue more secure and lucrative careers in the cities. The region has suffered many a viticultural crisis arising from the twin problems of over-production and mediocrity. Those days, it seems, are nearly over. There's one caveat in this rosy tale. The market for *vins doux naturels* is in decline. Lots of explanations are offered, like changing fashions or stricter drink-driving laws. Names like Rivesaltes and Maury will

BELOW *The Castillet, a Perpignan landmark.*

LOCAL INFORMATION

Office de Tourisme
Palais des Congres
66000 Perpignan
Tel: 04 68 66 30 30
Fax: 04 69 66 30 26

━━━━━ Côtes du Roussillon
Follow one of the three river
routes to sample the best of
the area

Côtes du Roussillon

Côtes du Roussillon-Villages

Maury

never disappear from the *cavistes'* shelves though – the market may be shrinking but the wines are delicious.

How to get there

Discovering Perpignan is best done by foot but to discover the wine country around Perpignan you'll need a car. The bus services are reliable but infrequent and cycling means long, hot uphill stretches often against 80km/hr (55 mile/hr) winds. Finding your way around is easy. Roussillon's three river valleys plot your routes.

Travelling around

Many top producers are located up the first of Roussillon's long valleys, the Agly. Having visited Château Roussillon to the east of Perpignan, take the D117 out of the city, heading for Rivesaltes, and then follow the river through some of Roussillon's

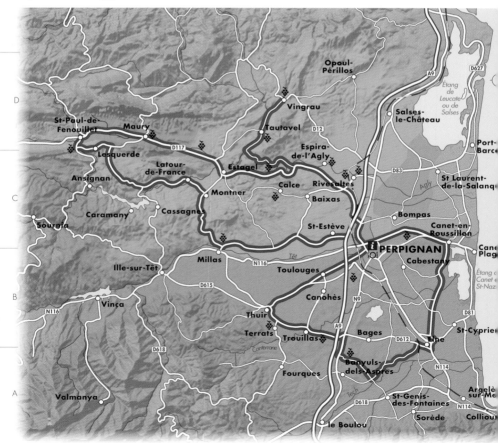

most delightful countryside. This route passes Cathar castles and takes in numerous pretty wine villages, like Estagel – visit the delightful Château de Jau before you head for lively Place Arago in Estagel. The D616 out of Perpignan, heading for Millas, follows the second of Roussillon's river valleys, the Têt. The main attractions along the Têt Valley include the fabulous rock formations, Les Orgues, at Ille-sur-Têt, and the fortified, walled town of Villefranche-de-Conflent, west of Prades.

The N114 takes you south, out of Perpignan, to Roussillon's other top producers – located between the Têt and the third river valley, the Tech. Check out the environmentally friendly Domaine Sarda-Malet. Other main attractions along the way are the fabulous cloisters at Elne cathedral and Roussillon's many Romanesque churches and chapels. Plan to spend at least three days discovering Roussillon's wine country.

What the wines are like

Two-thirds of the wines are big, concentrated and fruity reds, rosés and whites. The remainder is luscious *vins doux naturels* – France's first appellation wines, granted AC status in 1936 (Muscat de Rivesaltes followed in 1956). The Côtes du Roussillon appellation was created in 1977. The red only Côtes du Roussillon-Villages appellation covers the Agly Valley to the north of the *department*. Four villages can add their name to this label: Caramany, Tautavel, Latour-de-France and Lesquerde. The "Villages" designation is supposed to be a mark of superiority but it's the individual *vigneron* that really counts. The sweet *vins doux naturels* include Rivesaltes, Muscat de

ABOVE *Mt. Canigou, only 50km (30 miles) from the Mediterranean, dominates Roussillon's plane.*

GROWERS IN COTE DE ROUSSILLON AND RIVESALTES

Domaine Boudau
66600 Rivesaltes
Tel: 04 68 64 45 37 *(C3)*

Domaine Cazes
4 rue Francisco Ferrer
66002 Rivesaltes
Tel: 04 68 64 08 26 *(C3)*

Domaine Gauby
Le Faradjal
66600 Calce
Tel: **04 68 64 35 19** *(C3: moderate to expensive)*

Domaine Fontanel
25 ave Jean Jaurès
66720 Tautavel
Tel: 04 68 29 04 71 *(D3)*

Domaine Piquemal
66600 Espira-de-l'Agly
Tel: 04 68 64 09 14 *(C3)*

PRICES: *inexpensive to moderate* (other than where specified)

ABOVE *Sculpture in a cloister in the town of Elme.*

RIGHT *Château Barrera, one of Roussillon's dynamic producers.*

Rivesaltes and Maury. Three Rivesaltes styles exist – Ambré, Tuilé, and Grenat – distinguished by colour, grape varieties, and length of ageing. They can keep for decades. The pale gold Muscat de Rivesaltes is made from two grapes: the exotic Muscat à Petits Grains and the more citrus-flavoured Muscat d'Alexandrie. It should be drunk young. The black-cherry- and chocolate-flavoured Maury is based on Grenache Noir. It can be dark orange or mahogany in colour and keeps for decades. Some styles, often labelled *récolte*, are made to be drunk young. A pear-flavoured white Maury from Grenache Blanc also exists and should be enjoyed young.

Top growers in Côtes du Roussillon (see also p.139)

Château de Jau
RN 117, 66600 Casas-de-Pène, tel: 04 68 38 90 10, daure@wanadoo.fr
Before the Revolution, Cistercian monks worked what is now the Daure family's large estate between Casas-de-Pène and Estagel. Tautavel's medieval tower overlooks the grand pink château and in the courtyard there's a living historic monument, a magnificent 300-year-old mulberry tree. Enjoy the easy-drinking Jaja ("plonk") range but take home the top Syrah and Mourvèdre, Talon Rouge. In between, there's something for every taste. These are stylish, well-made wines. Between June and September, eat at Le Grill du Château de Jau and visit the contemporary art exhibition. (*C3: inexpensive to expensive*)

Château du Mas Déu
66300 Trouillas, tel: 04 68 53 11 66
Mansus Déi was the first Templar *commanderie* in Roussillon, established in 1138. The method by which *vins doux naturels* are still made was developed here in the thirteenth century by Montpellier alchemist and physician Arnaldus de Villanova. The alchemist-in-residence today is young Claude Olivier, ably assisted by parents Andréu-Jordi and Claudie. It is set in parkland just outside Trouillas on the Bages road. Tastethe characterful red Fûts de Chêne bottling, and for early drinking buy Cuvée Galdric. Look for the barrel-aged white Côtes du Roussillon and fruity Rivesaltes too. Admired by American Presidents and British Prime Ministers. (*B3: inexpensive to moderate*)

Domaine Laporte
Château Roussillon, 66000 Perpignan, tel: 04 68 50 06 53, domaine-laporte@wanadoo.fr
The Laporte family bought this attractive property with its distinctive round tower in 1962. It stands on the Roman site of

---

GROWERS CONTINUED

· ·

**Domaine des Chênes
Razungles et Fils**
66600 Vingrau
Tel: 04 68 29 40 21 *(D3: moderate)*

Domaine de la Coume du Roy
66460 Maur
Tel: 04 68 59 67 58 *(D2: moderate to expensive)*

Domaine Força-Réal
66170 Millas
Tel: 04 68 85 06 07 *(C2: inexpensive to moderate)*

Château Planères
66300 St-Jean-Lasseille
Tel: 04 68 21 74 50 *(A/B4: inexpensive to moderate)*

Mas Amiel
66460 Maury
Tel: 04 68 29 01 02 *(D2: moderate to expensive)*

Ruscino, the former capital of Roussillon, but only vestiges of the forum, baths, and amphitheatre remain. Since 1980, Patricia and Raymond Laporte have run the domaine and earned a reputation for exemplary *vins de pays, vins doux naturels* and a superior red Côtes du Roussillon. Their Syrah-based Domitia should be among your purchases. (*C4: moderate*)

Domaine Sarda-Malet
chemin de Ste-Barbe, 66000 Perpignan, tel: 04 68 56 72 38, www.sarda-malet.com
Suzy Malet, her late husband Max, and their son Jérôme transformed the nineteenth-century family estate on the river Têt after taking it over in 1983. They modernized the cellar and replanted, adding Syrah, Mourvèdre, Marsanne, Roussanne, and Viognier, while retaining the old vines. The environment is respected and natural methods are followed in the *cave*. Yields are very low for their top Terroir Mailloles red and white wines. Their basic Tradition is also admirable and in between there's the superb Réserve. They also make exceptional *vins doux naturels*. (*B4: inexpensive to expensive*)

Finding a place to stay
Perpignan is a good base and there are lots of accommodation options. Inexpensive hotels are on avenue Général de Gaulle near the train station and smarter ones are along the promenade des Plantanes near the tourist office. The three-star Hôtel de la Loge is centrally located in an attractive sixteenth-century building. The nearby two-star La Poste et Perdix is a charming nineteenth-century hotel near the Perpignan landmark of Castillet. Outside Perpignan, near Thuir, there's the Casa del Arte guesthouse with a swimming pool. Eating in Perpignan can be very cosmopolitan, but locals often lunch at the La Carmagnole *tarterie* – and show up early for this tiny institution. For dinner, try the superb organic Italian cuisine at Il Bambino (book ahead). And, try the Château de Jau grill. If you're out and about in Le Boulou, stop at Edouard Gomez's friendly tea room where you can buy chocolates, cakes, and ice-creams from this award-winning *patissier*.

WHERE TO STAY AND EAT

Hôtel de la Loge
1 rue Fabriques-Nabot
66000 Perpignan
Tel: 04 68 34 41 02

Il Bambino
25 rue Grande La Réal
66000 Perpignan
Tel: 04 68 34 41 30

La Carmagnole
12 rue de la Révolution
Française
66000 Perpignan
Tel: 04 68 35 44 46

La Casa del Arte
66300 Thuir
Tel: 04 68 53 44 78

Edouard Gomez
54 ave Du Général de
Gaulle
66160 Le Boulou
Tel: 04 68 83 16 38

La Poste et Perdix
6 rue Fabriques-Nabot
66000 Perpignan
Tel: 04 68 34 42 53

Collioure and Banyuls

The last vineyards in France before the Spanish border cover an amazing network of ancient, stony terraces along the spectacular Côte Vermeille, where the Pyrénées meet the Mediterranean. These are the vineyards of the small but prestigious Collioure and Banyuls appellations, named after two of the oldest and prettiest fishing villages in France. Collioure is still an important source of anchovies, which feature in Catalan salads and fish soups. Port-Vendres, between the two villages, hosts the main fish market today. Henri Matisse and the Fauvists put Collioure on the map at the start of the twentieth century and it remains a centre for art and artists. Collioure wines are white, rosé and red while those of Banyuls are red and white *vins doux naturels*. If you're in Banyuls during the last weekend in October, don't miss the grape harvest celebrations on the beach.

WHERE TO STAY AND EAT

Casa Pairal
Impasse des Palmiers
66190 Collioure
Tel: 04 68 82 05 81

Hôtel le Manoir
20 ave Marechal Joffre
66650 Banyuls-sur-Mer
Tel: 04 68 88 32 98

La Littorine
Plage Elmes
66650 Banyuls-sur-Mer
Tel: 04 68 88 03 12

Le Poisson Rouge
route de la Jetée
66660 Port-Vendres
Tel: 04 68 98 03 12

Les Templiers
quai de l'Amirante
Tel: 04 68 98 31 10

A fading fashion

There's debate over who first cultivated vines on the steep terraces above Collioure and Banyuls, on what's also known as La Côte Rocheuse ("the rocky coast"). Their origins probably go back to antiquity. The Templars are known to have extended the network of dry-stone walls and rainwater drains, nicknamed *les peus de gall* ("the chicken feet"), in the thirteenth century. These protect the terraces and prevent erosion during occasional heavy downpours in spring and autumn.

Today, it's unlikely that production of Collioure and Banyuls will increase, as space is limited. In fact, some *vignerons* are reducing Banyuls output and increasing the production of Collioure wines to meet demand as the fashion for *vins doux naturels* wanes – the wines come from the same vineyards. Curiously, Collioure used to be known as Banyuls Sec and was made strictly for local consumption in the days when *vins doux naturels* were more popular.

Like Roussillon's other *vins doux naturels*, Banyuls was one of the first wines in France granted appellation status (in 1936). Collioure's red wines earned their AC label in 1971, over a decade before neighbouring Languedoc's appellations (with the exception of Fitou).

What the wines are like

It's the combination of mountain and sea influences that gives Collioure and Banyuls wines their concentration, character and distinctiveness. Collioure wines come in all three colours and they tend to be full bodied. The reds are sometimes compared to those of Châteauneuf-du-Pape and they're generally good for keeping a decade. The rosés are robust too, and really made to accompany food. The whites are aromatic and flavourful.

Banyuls wines seem to come in no end of styles and include red and white, though pink and mahogany exist too. It all depends on the blend of grape varieties, the method of vinification – notably whether the wine has been oxidized and taken on the so-called (and much sought-after) *rancio* tang – and the age of the wine. Generally speaking, there's the young *rimage* version and then the older styles, some of which are aged in glass demijohns (or *bonbonnes*) that you'll see sitting around exposed to the elements. Depending on the style, Banyuls wines accompany blue cheeses, pastries, pâtés, and even chocolate.

Travelling around (*see* map p.132)

You can base yourself in either Banyuls-sur-Mer or Collioure and then visit producers on foot: most are signposted. You'll need a car to travel the winding coast road between the towns or to head up into the steep hills where the vineyards are found, as it's rare to see cyclists or walkers attempting either route. If

LOCAL INFORMATION

Office de Tourisme
Place du 18 Juin
66190 Collioure
Tel: 04 68 82 15 47
www.little-france.com/
collioure

OVERLEAF *The beautiful Château Valmy just outside Argelès-sur-Mer (see p.133).*

BELOW *The port of Collioure, reaching from sea to mountains.*

you're based in Perpignan, there are trains and buses to Collioure and Banyuls.

The best place to begin the Côte Vermeille wine route is just outside Argelès-sur-Mer at beautiful Château Valmy. The views over the vineyards to the sea are spectacular. From Valmy, take the stunning Corniche road to Collioure. You can stop at a number of picnic spots along the way and enjoy the views. Energetic types will want to drive up, and then walk the final leg, to Tour Madeloc above Collioure. You can take in the entire Côte Vermeille from this spot. There's a lot to see in busy little Collioure when not tasting wines at domaines like La Tour Vieille and Piétri-Géraud, so plan to spend a few hours looking around. From Collioure, follow the Corniche road to Port-Vendres, leaving time for Les Clos de Paulilles before heading into Banyuls-sur-Mer. The Cap Béar peninsula south of Port-Vendres is worth a detour. Banyuls offers plenty to choose from, including the enterprising Domaine de la Coume del Mas, the superlative Domaine Vial-Magnères, and the organic Domaine Traginer. Banyuls may be the last wine town on the route, but a trip further south to Cerbère, the last village before Spain, covers some spectacular coastal scenery. You can explore Collioure and Banyuls in a couple of days, but you'll want to stay longer in this beautiful region.

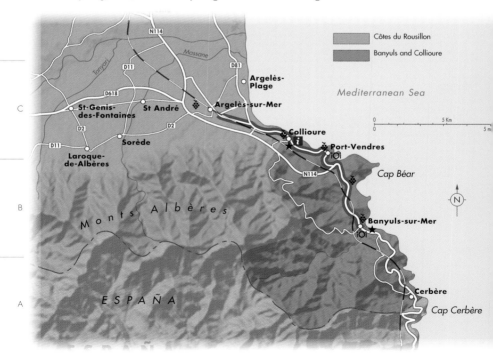

Top growers to visit (*see also* p.140)

Château Valmy

66700 Argelès-sur-Mer, tel: 04 68 81 25 70,
chateau.valmy@free.fr
This elegant, white nineteenth-century château and luxury hotel
in the Albères foothills overlooks the village of Argelès-sur-Mer
and the long sandy beach where the Côte Vermeille begins.
Bernard and Martine Carbonnell have modernized the cellars
and replanted the vineyards. Producing superior expressions of
the Côtes du Roussillon appellation, some of their top wines are
vins de pays. Look for the rich white Les Roses Blanches, the
oaked Syrah Le Premier, and delicious Rivesaltes. (*C2: moderate*)

Domaine de la Coume del Mas

66300, Banyuls-sur-Mer, tel: 04 68 88 37 03
The story of Coume del Mas began with a wager. The bet was
whether a young band of *vignerons* could produce wines that
would stand out at a tasting of young wines in Bordeaux. When
their red Collioure Quadratur and Banyuls Quintessence
wowed the judges, the bet was considered won. Now this
dynamic group has an agreement with the Cave de l'Abbé
Rous co-op in Banyuls to use the latter's top-class cellars. Look
for these wines and the excellent red Schistes and white Folio.
Call ahead and don't miss out. (*B4: moderate to expensive*)

Finding a place to stay

Accommodation in either town is hard to find in summer so
book ahead. In Collioure, the three-star Casa Pairal is a grand
hotel with garden and pool in the centre. Alternatively, the
characterful two-star Les Templiers is where Picasso stayed. In
Banyuls, the Hôtel le Manoir is a simple, cosy and inexpensive
option in the centre. Dining along the coast inevitably means
seafood. The Poisson Rouge in Port-Vendres is below a ruined
fort on the lighthouse side of the port with a terrace next to the
water. In Banyuls, La Littorine is one of Roussillon's best eateries.

Other things to do

Collioure landmarks include the church of Notre-Dame-des-
Anges with its fabulous *reredos* (altarpiece) and famous bell
tower, and the beautiful Maison Pams, now a museum of
contemporary art. You can follow in the footsteps of Matisse and
others along the chemin des Fauves and have a drink where
most of them stayed, at Les Templiers, where paintings adorn the
walls. In Banyuls, head out of town 4km (2.5 miles) to the
Musée Maillol at Mas La Baillaurie where this sculptor of
young, fleshy Mediterranean women lived and worked. Back in
town, head for the *cave* of the Les Templiers co-op for an
introduction to *vins doux naturels*.

GROWERS IN COLLIOURE AND BANYULS

Les Clos de Paulilles
66660 Port-Vendres
Tel: 04 68 38 90 10
Located on a beautiful,
protected site on the coast
between Port-Vendres and
Banyuls with its own cove
and restaurant. A good
source of Collioure and
Banyuls wine, and gourmet
vinegar, too. (*C3: moderate*)

Domaine Claire Mayol
Quai Forgas
66660 Port-Vendres
Two young *vignerons* run
this winery. Old Rivesaltes
is a speciality, besides
good-value Banyuls and
Collioure. (*C3: inexpensive*)

Domaine Piétri-Géraud
22 rue Pasteur
66190 Collioure
Tel: 04 68 82 07 42
Maguy Piétri-Géraud and
her daughter Laetitia run
this estate with cellars in
the centre of Collioure.
Their Banyuls wines are
particularly good. (*C3:
moderate*)

Domaine de la Rectorie
54 ave du Puig del Mas
66650 Banyuls-sur-Mer
Brothers Thierry and Marc
Parcé make three excellent
and different Collioure
reds: Col del Blast, Le Seris
and Coume Pascole. Look
for the fine white Argile,
too. (*B4: expensive*)

Domaine Vial-Magnères
Clos St-André
14 rue Edouard Herriot
66650 Banyuls-sur-Mer
Tel: 04 68 88 31 04
Arguably the best source
of white Banyuls. The red
Collioure, Les Espérades,
and old *rancio* Banyuls,
Al Tragou, deserve a
mention. (*B4: moderate*)

Best buys from top producers

A selection of some of the finest producers worth tracking down in the south of France follows. Where mentioned, the map reference refers to the map in the relevant main section.

NICE AND BELLET

Château de Bellet
Les Séoules, 06200 Nice
Tel: 04 93 37 81 57
A terracotta-coloured château with twin towers and seventeenth-century chapel set in parkland with views over the Var Valley and the Alps. Arguably the appellation's driving force, Ghislain de Charnacé's family has been in Bellet for four centuries and he is president of the Bellet *syndicat*. de Charnacé is a strong advocate of Braquet and makes a pure Braquet rosé, plus long-lasting reds based on the grape. He has two excellent white *cuvées* from Rolle, one unoaked and the other, Baron G, fermented and matured in oak. Deservedly pricey. *(B2: expensive)*

Château Crémat
M. et Mme. Kamerbeek
442 chemin de Crémat
06200 Nice
Tel: 04 92 15 12 15
The recent history of the estate has been uncertain but the latest owners have engaged a new winemaker, which augurs well. The reds are made to cellar a good ten years or more. If you buy just one bottle, pick up the aromatic barrel-aged Rolle-based white. *(Map p.44, B2: moderate to expensive)*

COTES DE PROVENCE

Château des Garcinières
RN98, 83310 Cogolin
Tel: 04 94 56 02 85
www.chateau-garcinieres.com
A grand avenue of plane trees

leads to this twelfth-century Cistercian abbey converted in the eighteenth century into the Count of Grimaldi's majestic residence. Two *cuvées* exist in pink and red, both exemplary, the Traditionnelle and the superior Cuvée du Prieure. All whites are Traditionnelle. *(inexpensive to moderate)*

Château de St-Martin
route des Arcs
83460 Taradeau
Tel: 04 94 99 76 76
chateausaintmartin@free.fr
An eighteenth-century *bastide* with twelfth-century cellars where the Provençal *cru classé* designation was born. Boasting the remains of a Roman villa, a chapel and an English park, ask to see the *son et lumière* presentation and buy the Tibouren-based rosés, powerful old-vine oaked reds, and elegant whites. *(moderate)*

Château St-Maur
83310 Cogolin
Tel: 04 94 54 63 12
A splendid nineteenth-century *cru classé* estate between Grimaud and Cogolin, this bottled its first wine in 1922. The attractive buildings alone are worth the visit. Rosé is important here. The pinks are aged in vats for eight months and are made for Provençal cuisine. This is also where to find flavoursome, complex reds aged for eighteen months in barrels. *(Map p.49, C2: moderate to expensive)*

Domaine de la Bastide Neuve
83340 Le Cannet-des-Maures
Tel: 04 94 50 09 80

Oenologue Jérôme Paquette runs this star domaine east of Le Cannet. He uses traditional Provençal barrels called *boutes*, larger than Bordeaux barriques, to make wines in three colours. The red Cuvée d'Antan is matured in *boutes* and will develop over a decade. *(moderate)*

Domaine les Fouques
Hameau Bastide
1er Borrels, 83400 Hyères
Tel: 04 94 35 25 30
fouques.bio@wanadoo.fr
This Biodynamic domaine in Le Pradet produces well-made wines at pocket-friendly prices. Enjoy them over a meal on the domaine's terrace with views over the vineyards, the sea and the Ile de Porquerolles. The homespun gastronomy uses fresh vegetables from the domaine's organic garden. *(inexpensive)*

Domaine Gavoty
Le Grand Campdumy
83340 Cabasse
Tel: 04 94 69 72 39
domaine.gavoty@wanadoo.fr
A seventeenth-century *bastide* which has been in the same family for 200 years and produces an impressive range of wines. The Tradition range represents good value for money but the Cuvée Clarendon range is the star. The Syrah/Cabernet rosés are some of the finest around. *(inexpensive to moderate)*

Domaine du Jas d'Esclans
3094 route Callas
83920 La Motte
Tel: 04 98 10 29 29

A good-value, organic *cru classé* estate in a beautiful setting. Reds spend two years in oak foudres. Look for the almost pure Clairette Cuvée du Loup, one of the best whites around. New owners (in 2002) promise to continue the domaine's traditions. *(inexpensive to moderate)*

Domaine de Rimauresq
route Notre-Dame-des-Anges, 83790 Pignans
Tel: 04 94 48 80 45
www.rimauresq.com
This Scottish-owned *cru classé* estate makes an uncomplicated range and has a reputation for oak-aged reds, Tibouren rosés, and a superior Rolle-based white. Its wines are a benchmark for quality in the Côtes de Provence. "R." belongs to the superior range. *(moderate)*

Domaine de la Sanglière
3886 route Léoube
Tel: 04 94 00 48 58
This unpretentious domaine on the Brégançon peninsula makes two good-value *cuvées*. The basic Maison and the superior Cuvée Spéciale. *(inexpensive to moderate)*

COTEAUX VAROIS
Cellier de la Ste Baume
RN7, 83470 St-Maximin
Tel: 04 94 78 03 97
This *cave coopérative* is known as the Amicale to its 300 members. It's an old co-op with typical Provençal architecture and a good place to find top-value wines in all three colours. The top red is the Cuvée Spéciale. *(inexpensive)*

Château Margillière
route de Cabasse
83170 Brignoles
Tel: 04 94 69 05 34
This charming *bastide* makes a substantial Rolle-Ugni Blanc AC, a generous AC red, a sparkling white, and a fun

bag-in-box range. *(B2: inexpensive to moderate)*

Domaine du Deffends
83470 St-Maximin
Tel: 04 94 78 03 91
Has wonderful views. Try the delicious Viognier-Rolle, and buy the *foudre*-aged Syrah-Cabernet Clos de la Truffière. *(Map p.53, C4: inexpensive to moderate)*

Domaine Fontainebleau
route de Mont-Fort, D22, Le Val
Tel: 04 94 59 59 09
One of the region's most idyllic properties. Buy the fullsome rosé. *(C2: inexpensive to moderate)*

Domaine du Loou
D5, 83136
La Roquebrussanne
Tel: 04 94 86 94 97
You pass the remains of a Roman villa discovered when replanting at this estate, where traditional, well-structured reds based on Syrah are emphasized. It also has some thirty-year-old Cabernet and even older Mourvèdre. For whites there's Rolle and Sémillon. *(inexpensive)*

BANDOL AND CASSIS
Château de Fontcreuse
13 route de la Ciotal
13260 Cassis
Tel: 04 42 01 71 09
This beautifully restored seventeenth-century winery belongs to the president of the Cassis *syndicat* and not surprisingly it's one of the star estates. Jean-François Brando runs a thoroughly modern operation and produces a big crisp white Cassis and an ample rosé from Cinsault and Grenache. He doesn't make reds because that's not what Cassis is about. *(Map p.57, B3: moderate)*

Château de Pibarnon
410 chemin de la Croix-des-Signaux
83470 La Cadière d'Azur
Tel: 04 94 90 12 73
This fabulous estate is the highest in the appellation and overlooks an amphitheatre of vines, pines, and *garrigue*. Comte Henri de St-Victor liked the Bandol he drank in a local restaurant while on holiday here so much that he bought this place in 1977. He now produces one of the top Bandol reds, plus a rosé worthy of ageing and an appealing white. The wines benefit from the estate's peculiar geology that gives particularly elegant tannins. *(B2: expensive)*

Château Romassan
601 route des Mourvèdres
83330 Le Castellet
Tel: 04 94 98 71 91
This pretty Ott family estate is famous for the sought-after Coeur de Grain rosé. Also, big reds and a crisp Sauvignon-based white. *(B2: expensive)*

Château Salettes
83740 La Cadière d'Azur
Tel: 04 94 90 06 06
www.salettes.com
This grand old property has been in the Ricard family for 400 years, and the cellars date back to 1677. The seventeenth generation runs the place today. The Ricards' red is surprisingly supple for a Bandol. *(moderate)*

Clos d'Albizzi
Ferme St-Vincent
ave des Albizzi
13260 Cassis
Tel: 04 42 01 11 43
François Dumont is a descendent of the Albizzis, who founded this estate in 1523. Buy his white Cassis and drink it now or keep for up to a decade. *(moderate)*

Domaine Caillol
11 chemin de Bérard
13260 Cassis
Tel: 04 42 01 05 35
This simple, traditional
domaine makes excellent
and affordable whites. The
top Blanc de Blancs stresses
Marsanne. As with other
small domaines, ring ahead.
(inexpensive to moderate)

Domaine de la Ferme Blanche
route de Marseille
RD559, 13260 Cassis
Tel: 04 42 01 00 74
The largest and one of the
oldest family domaines in
Cassis. François Paret makes
a white from all five permitted
varieties and a rich Blanc de
Blancs from Marsanne and
Clairette. *(moderate)*

Domaine La Suffrène
1066 chemin de Cuges
83740 La Cadière d'Azur
Tel: 04 94 90 09 23
www.domaine-la-suffrene.com
This charming old family
domaine produces a range
of well-made wines. The top
red is the Cuvée des Lauves
and the top rosé is the Cuvée
Ste-Catherine. Both are
exemplary. The white also
packs a punch. *(inexpensive
to moderate)*

La Roque
Quartier Vallon
83470 La Cadière d'Azur
Tel: 04 94 90 10 39
www.laroque-bandol.fr
This Bandol co-op is the place
to find astonishingly
affordable and well made
appellation wines in all three
colours. Look for the attractive
bottles with the French
Impressionist labels.
(inexpensive)

Moulin des Costes
BP 17
83740 La Cadière d'Azur
Tel: 04 94 98 58 98
www.bunan.com

This leading producer makes
immediately accessible reds
and a superior château red
from a parcel of fifty-year-
old Mourvèdre. The family's
Château la Rouvière wines
are more expensive while the
Moulin wines are lighter.
(moderate)

STE-VICTOIRE
Château Ferry Lacombe
route de St-Maximin
13530 Trets
Tel: 04 42 29 40 04
www.ferrylacombe.com
This attractive *bergerie* is on
the flanks of Mount Aurélien
just outside Trets. All three
colours are produced under
two labels, the superior Cuvée
Lou Cascaï, and Les Hauts de
Lacombe. The Lou Cascaï
Clairette is perfect as an
apéritif or with food.
(moderate)

COTEAUX D'AIX-EN-PROVENCE
Château Bas
13116 Vernègues
Tel: 04 90 59 13 16
www.chateaubas.com
A seventeenth-century estate
outside Vernègues and one of
the most beautiful in the area.
The 86ha vineyard produces
a variety of wines, including
a sparkling Ugni Blanc-
Sauvignon blend. The wines,
in order of excellence, include
the good-value L'Alvernègue,
the Pierres du Sud, and the
Cuvée du Temple. *(Map p.66,
B3: inexpensive to moderate)*

COSTIERES DE NIMES
Château de Campuget
RD403, 30129 Manduel
Tel: 04 66 20 20 15
www.campuget.com
www.chateaulamarine.com
This modern outfit produces
reliable, good-value wines.
The premium Château de
L'Amarine wines come
from the family's Bellegarde
vineyards, like the top white
Cuvée Bernis. The best

Château de Campuget red
is the La Sommelière.
(inexpensive to moderate)

TERRASSES DU LARZAC
Mas Cal Demoura
34725 Jonquières
Tel: 04 67 88 61 51
Jean-Pierre Jullien's Mas Cal
Demoura is next door to his
son Olivier's Mas Jullien. This
is a smaller operation and,
except for an exchange of
views, it's quite independent
from Mas Jullien. Buy his
excellent oaked red Coteaux
du Languedoc. *(moderate)*

FAUGERES
Domaine St-Antonin
Hameau de La Liquière
34480 Cabrerolles
Tel: 04 67 90 13 24
Frédéric Albaret is an
independent-minded,
passionate winemaker. He
makes just two red wines in
his small *cave* in La Liquinère.
The Tradition and the oaked
Magnous. These wines belong
in your cellar. *(moderate)*

ST-CHINIAN
Château La Dournie
34360 St-Chinian
Tel: 04 67 38 19 43
chateau.ladournie@
libertysurf.fr
This attractive property is
set in mature parkland on
the edge of St-Chinian. The
Etienne family have been here
for seven generations. Their
St-Chinian reds are based
on Syrah, and the top red is
oaked. They are good-value
examples of the appellation.
(inexpensive to moderate)

MINERVOIS
Château Bonhomme
11800 Aigues-Vives
Tel: 04 68 79 28 48
Fans of full-bodied, potent
and fruity reds should buy
Jean-Pierre Aimar's organic
Minervois. Les Alaternes is his
top red with lots of old-vine
Carignan, while Les Oliviers

emphasizes low-yielding Syrah. *(inexpensive to moderate)*

Château Coupe Roses
rue Poterie
34210 La Caunette
Tel: 04 68 91 21 95
coupe-roses@wanadoo.fr
An old family estate, with vineyards perched on slopes around the troglodyte village of La Caunette. The pretty name refers to red bricks that used to be cut from the hillsides. Buy the Calvez's red Les Plots, Prestige, and Orience – they're great value wines. *(inexpensive)*

Château Fabas
11800 Laure-Minervois
Tel: 04 68 78 17 82
A former Moët et Chandon director shows what you can do with Vermentino and oak with his *cuvée* Virginie here. His stylish red *cuvée* Alexandre also gets oak. *(moderate to expensive)*

Château Gibalaux-Bonnet
11800 Laure-Minervois
Tel: 04 68 78 12 02
www.gibalauxbonnet.com
The Bonnets' property, a former priory of Caunes Abbey, is spread out over the sun-baked Balcons de l'Aude between Trèbes and Laure-Minervois. Buy their red or white Cuvée Prieuré. *(inexpensive to moderate)*

Château La Grave
11800 Badens
Tel: 04 68 79 16 00
chateaulagrave@wanadoo.fr
The Orosquettes are friendly folk who have a special affection for their old Macabeu. They make two great whites from it: the floral Expression and oaked Privilège. The good-value reds go by the same names. *(moderate)*

Château de Paraza
11200 Paraza
Tel: 04 68 43 20 76
www.chateau-de-paraza.com
This baronial chateau in tiny Paraza overlooks the Canal du Midi. Paul Riquet, the canal's architect, stayed here and built the terraces. Pop in and buy the Cuvée Spéciale. Don't miss the nearby Pont-Canal that carries the canal over the river Répudre. It's the oldest canal bridge in France. *(inexpensive)*

Château Russol
11800 Laure-Minervois
Tel: 04 68 78 17 68
www.chateau-russol.com
You can take a walking tour of this fascinating estate that boasts a 5,000 year-old dolmen that's one of the finest in Europe. Then buy the Grande Réserve Pallax; it's a top Syrah-based red Minervois. Look for the late-harvested Viognier and a Minervois Noble, too. *(moderate)*

Domaine La Tour Boisée
BP3, 11800 Laure-Minervois
Tel: 04 68 78 10 04
www.domainelatourboisee.com
La Tour Boisée is an impressive collection of old grey stone buildings surrounded by Aleppo pines. Jean-Louis Poudou's best red is the Cuvée Marielle et Frédérique; his top white is the Cuvée Marie-Claude. Look for the botrytized Chardonnay in the slender bottle, too. *(inexpensive)*

MALEPERE
Château de Cointes
11290 Roullens
Tel: 04 68 26 81 05
www.chateaudecointes.com
The Gorostis' simple range of well-made Malepère wines includes two reds and a rosé. Buy the top red, Croix du Languedoc, with its attractive art-deco label.

The *cave* is open in the mornings; call ahead at other times. *(inexpensive)*

Château de Robert
11150 Villesiscle
Tel: 04 68 76 11 86
www.chateauderobert.com
Marie-Hélène Merail-Artigouha is the latest in a line of women to take the reins at this splendid château on the west flank of the Malepère Massif. She says the Rhône inspires her but her well-made wines are more like rather rustic Bordeaux. *(inexpensive)*

Château de Routier
17 ave Madailhan
11240 Routier
Tel: 04 68 69 06 13
chateau-de-routier.vins-malepere.com
A grand fifteenth-century château with two round towers and a mini-museum of viticulture in its medieval, vaulted cellars. The energetic Michèle Lezerat took over the family estate in the 1980s. She's replanted the vineyards and stresses the Bordeaux varieties in her red Malepère and makes three *cuvées* plus some white *vins de pays* and a rosé. The reds are either for early drinking (Eloïse), for the medium-term (La Damoiselle), or for keeping (chunky La Renaissance). The latter spends two years in oak. Try the oaked Chardonnay too. *(inexpensive)*

CABARDES
Château de Pennautier
11610 Pennautier
Tel: 04 68 72 65 29
www.vignobles-lorgeril.com
A magnificent seventeenth-century château with gardens by Le Nôtre. One of three fine Cabardès properties belonging to the Lorgeril family. Vineyards overlook the Montagne Noire, the Pyrénées, and Carcassonne.

A well-made range of wines includes a choice of varietal *vins de pays*. The best wines are the Cabardès. Look for Collection Privée and L'Esprit de Pennautier. The former uses Bordeaux grapes and spends fourteen months in oak; the latter has mostly Syrah and spends eighteen months in oak. There are some curiosities, such as Le Rêve de Pennautier: late-harvested, oak-aged, sweet Chardonnay. Super stuff. *(moderate)*

LIMOUX
Domaine de L'Aigle
11300 Roquetaillade
Tel: 04 68 31 56 72.
www.rodet.com
The Burgundy négociant Antonin Rodet recently bought this estate high up in the wild and windy hills southwest of Limoux. The name means "Eagle's Domaine" and the sign claims that it is "France's best mountain vineyard". Rodet was impressed by the location and the performance of Pinot Noir and Chardonnay in this cool island in the south. He makes excellent still and sparkling Limoux wines and some red *vins de pays* from Pinot Noir. Don't miss out. *(Map p.113, B3: moderate)*

Domaine La Batteuse
11 route de Couiza
11190 Antugnac
Tel: 04 68 74 21 02
Bernard Delmas makes a rich and flavourful *crémant* at this organic domaine with, one suspects, more Chardonnay than the regulations permit. His Blanquette is also hugely satisfying. *(B3: inexpensive to moderate)*

Domaine Martinolles
Etablissements Vergnes
11250 St-Hilaire
Tel: 04 68 69 41 93
www.martinolles.fr
The Vergnes' domaine in St-Hilaire is one of the

appellation's biggest estates. They go for low yields and make an excellent Ancestrale from old Mauzac vines. They're also fans of Pinot Noir, making an oaked version that shouldn't be missed. They also have a *gîte* for five people. *(inexpensive to moderate)*

Jean-Louis Denois
11300 Roquetaillade
Tel: 04 68 31 39 12
Jean-Louis Denois didn't sell the whole farm to Rodet: he kept around 5ha of vines plus the *cave* and house. He doesn't believe that Mauzac performs well here so he makes a sparkling wine along Champagne lines with Chardonnay and Pinot Noir. He also makes arguably the best Chardonnay in Limoux, a wine that will improve with ageing. His Pinot Noir *vin de pays* is a luscious alternative to Burgundy. Denois also buys in grapes from other growers and makes a juicy Merlot and a warm Carignan. Telephone ahead. *(B3: moderate)*

CORBIERES
Château St-Auriol
11220 Lagrasse
Tel: 04 68 43 29 50
www.meschateaux.com
This lovely estate overlooks the Roman ruins of Villeberxas on the southern slopes of Montagne d'Alaric. The name refers to the gold sometimes found in springs on the estate. Buy the superior barrel-fermented whites and reds. *(moderate)*

Château La Baronne
Las Lanos
11700 Fontcouverte
Tel: 04 68 43 90 20
The Lignères are known for their white Corbières and they make a fine Gris de Gris. The reds, like the Montagne d'Alaric, are also well made. *(moderate)*

Château Grand Moulin
6 ave Gallieni
11200 Luc-sur-Orbieu
Tel: 04 68 27 40 80
chateaugrandmoulin@
wanadoo.fr
This fine property is set in beautiful countryside around Lézignan. Jean-Noël Bousquet emphasizes Mourvèdre in his Terres Rouges, Vieilles Vignes and exceptional Grand Millésime. He also makes two attractive whites. *(moderate)*

Château Lastours
11490 Portel-des-Corbières
Tel: 04 68 48 29 17
portelchateaudelastours@
wanadoo.fr
This large estate is frequently on the Paris-Dakar rally route. It's also a Centre d'Aide par le Travail, providing work for sixty handicapped people. Buy the top château red or the "Simone Descamps". There's accommodation and a fine restaurant, "La Bergerie", too. *(inexpensive to moderate)*

Château Les Ollieux
D6131, 1200 Montséret
Tel: 04 68 43 32 61
www.chateaulesollieux.com
The Cistercians founded France's first abbey for women here in 1153. The Surbézys bought the estate in 1855. They make three juicy reds: the basic Corbières, the Fûts de Chêne, and the superior Françoise Cartier. *(moderate)*

Château Les Palais
11220 St-Laurent-de-la-Cabrerisse
Tel: 04 68 44 01 63
The origins of this picturesque estate are religious rather than baronial. Today, the chapel is an attractive tasting room. The best of the Carignan-based *cuvées* is the excellent Randolin. *(inexpensive to moderate)*

Château Ventaillole
11610 Ventenac
Tel: 04 68 24 92 74
A historic estate within pines and garrigue. The organic-oriented Corbières winery emphasizes the Midi side of the Cabardès personality in its juicy château *cuvée*, which includes wine from old Grenache and Syrah vines. *(inexpensive)*

Château La Voulte-Gasparets
11200 Boutenac
Tel: 04 68 27 07 86
An attractive domaine and one of the region's stars and pioneers. Buy the Reverdys' Carignan-inspired reds (Cuvée Réservée) and the oaked, old-vine Romain Pauc. Don't miss the whites. *(moderate)*

Domaine du Grand Crès
ave de la Mer
11200 Ferrals-les-Corbières
Tel: 04 68 43 69 08
The Leferrers started with just 5ha in 1989 and over ten years replanted the vineyard parcel by parcel, adding 10ha. High-density planting and low yields typify their approach. They say their wines have a "northern" feel due to the altitude (300m/ 984 feet) and the owners' Burgundy background. Their modern cellar is in an old converted shepherd's barn in the village. Don't miss the red Majeure from low-yielding Syrah, the premium Cinsault rosé, and the aromatic white Corbières. Exemplary wines. *(Map p.118, C2: moderate to expensive)*

LA CLAPE
Château Pech-Céleyran
11110 Salles d'Aude
Tel: 04 68 33 50 04
www.pech-celeyran.com
This elegant château once belonged to the Toulouse-Lautrecs, and Henri's paintings of the place are at his Albi museum. Today, the St-

Exupérys make two succulent reds and a subtly oaked white La Clape. *(moderate)*

Château Pech-Redon
route de Gruissan
La Clape, 11200 Narbonne
Tel: 04 68 90 41 22
There's a long, winding track up to this estate near La Clape's summit. When you get there, buy Christophe Bousquet's rich white, famous rosé, and excellent-value red Les Cades. *(inexpensive to moderate)*

Domaine de l'Hospitalet
11100 Narbonne-Plage
Tel: 04 68 45 36 00
www.gerard-bertrand.com
This vast estate of rugby man and wine entrepreneur Gérard Bertrand boasts a stylish wine boutique, a museum, a courtyard arts and crafts "village", two restaurants, a twenty-two-room inn, and holiday *gîtes*. While you're there, buy the juicy La Clape Summum or Extrème. A speciality is the 'l'Hospitalène' apéritif. *(inexpensive to expensive)*.

FITOU
Domaine Bertrand Bergé
11530 Paziols
Tel: 04 68 45 41 73
Jérôme Bertrand produces luscious, rich, and characterful Fitou wines based on Carignan, Grenache Noir, and Syrah. His family have been *vignerons* here since 1911. Jérôme decided to renovate the cellar and make his own wines in 1993 and quickly established a reputation. Look for Ancestrale, a modern Fitou that includes Syrah, and Mégalithes, based on old-vine Carignan. The top wine, new Jean Sirven, has become a benchmark for Fitou. If you ask, he might show you around the cellars and the vineyards too. *(moderate)*

Domaine de Rolland
11350 Tuchan
Tel: 04 68 45 42 47
earlcolomer@aol.com
The cellars are contained in an old town house on the main square in Tuchan. Louis Colomer's Fitou emphasizes Carignan from old vines and low yields. The wind and sun concentrate the flavours and low rainfall limits yields. As a result, this is an excellent spot to find full-bodied, handmade wines. Look for the hearty Cuvée Spéciale from his oldest vines; it contains more Syrah than the basic Fitou. He doesn't oak his Fitou, as it already has enough tannin to keep it going for up to a decade. *(Map p.118, A2: moderate)*

COTES DU ROUSSILLON
Château Barrera
66407 Ste-Marie-la-Mer
Tel: 04 68 80 54 51
chateaubarrera@wanadoo.fr
An attractive Italianate château, not far from Roussillon's beaches. The Camargue-like terroir also produces artichokes and rice. Buy the superior red Côtes du Roussillon and the delicious, sweet Grand Roussillon. *(inexpensive)*

Domaine Ferrer Ribière
20 rue du Colombier
66300 Terrats
Tel: 04 68 53 24 45
In the foothills of Mount Canigou between Trouillas and Thuir, this estate is an unfaltering source of bold wines. Denis Ferrer and Bruno Ribière's approach to winemaking is straightforward: good grapes make good wines. They only grow Midi varieties but their output is pretty unconventional and thus mostly *vin de pays*. With 125-year-old Carignan they make a rich, rustic varietal. There's a varietal Grenache Gris and a Grenache Blanc too. Their

Mémoire des Temps is a daring Côtes du Roussillon. Sélénae is a top red to keep. One of their late-harvested sweet wines defies official classification. *(Map p.126, B3: moderate to expensive)*

Château St-Roch
66460 Maury
Tel: 04 68 29 07 20
A lovely old domaine – the pride and joy of Marc and Emma Bournazeau. Between Estagel and Maury, it is overlooked by Château Quéribus. Buy the superior Côtes du Roussillon reds and zesty rosé called "Pink". Don't miss the sweet white Maury, either. *(moderate)*

Domaine du Mas Crémat
66600 Espira de l'Agly
Tel: 04 68 38 92 06
Fax: 04 68 38 92 23
www.mascremat.com
Former Burgundians run this estate with its tastefully restored old farmhouse outside Espira de l'Agly. They practise sustainable, traditional viticulture and produce two top Côtes du Roussillon reds, one from their black schist vineyard and the other from limestone soils. Buy the excellent white La Yose, as well. *(moderate)*

Maison du Muscat
9 ave Gambetta
66600 Rivesaltes
Tel: 04 68 38 56 53
maison-du-muscat@
wanadoo.fr
Author and winemaker Henri Lhéritier's amazing emporium showcases over 100 different Muscat de Rivesaltes from Roussillon's best producers. The attractive shop is in a traditional

Catalan brick and stone building on the main square in Rivesaltes. *(inexpensive to expensive)*

COLLIOURE AND BANYULS
Domaine du Mas Blanc
9 ave du Général de Gaulle
66650 Banyuls-sur-Mer
Tel: 04 68 88 32 12
www.domaine-du-mas-blanc.com
This is where the Banyuls and Collioure appellations got their start. For two generations, the doctors Parcé (father and son) were the driving force behind the ACs. Today, Jean-Michel Parcé runs the family domaine, which dates back to 1639. Not surprisingly, he is a self-proclaimed member of the "old guard" and he's proud of being one of the most traditional domaines on the Côte Vermeille. The widely admired Collioure reds include Cosprons Levants, Clos du Moulin and Les Junquets. The first blends Syrah and Mourvèdre, the second emphasizes Mourvèdre and the last is mostly Syrah. More affordable reds include L'Agoulle and La Llose. The range of exceptional Banyuls includes André Parcé, aged fifteen years in *foudres*. *(expensive)*

Domaine La Tour Vieille
12 route de Madeloc
66190 Collioure
Tel: 04 68 82 44 82
An old, crenellated look-out tower stands over the La Tourette vineyard of this estate on the outskirts of Collioure. The property also has a vineyard high above Banyuls, called La Salette after the nearby white chapel that overlooks the village.

The two vineyards were united in 1982 with the marriage of Vincent Cantié and Christine Campadieu, from Collioure and Banyuls respectively. They produce wines in all three colours; they make two or three red *cuvées* depending on the vintage, naming them after vineyard parcels, like the top Puig Oriol, the Puig Ambeille and La Pinede. Their classy white is Les Canadells. They make excellent red and white Banyuls too, and a rarity called "Vin de Méditation" from a solera containing some decades-old wine. *(moderate)*

Domaine Traginer
56 ave du Puig del Mas
66650 Banyuls-sur-Mer
Tel: 04 68 88 15 11
www.traginer.com
This domaine's name means "mule-driver" in Catalan, for Jean-François Deu's small, organic vineyard is worked by hand with the aid of one of the last working mules in Banyuls. Not just for this have his wines attained a cult status; Deu is also passionate about quality and tradition. His vines are around forty-five years old and yields are tiny. His wines are vinified at picturesque Mas Atxer in the Banyuls back-country, but you can try them two minutes from the beach in Banyuls. They're concentrated, characterful and palate-bendingly complex. One of the top Collioure reds is the dense Cuvée d'Octobre. Any of his Banyuls wines are worth recommending. The Rimage is particularly satisfying. *(moderate)*

INDEX